SEX:
IT'S WORTH WAITING FOR

IT'S
WORTH
WAITING
FOR

by

GREG SPECK

MOODY PRESS
CHICAGO

All Scripture quotations in this publication are from the *Holy Bible: New International Version.* Copyright © 1973, 1977, 1984, International Bible Society. Used by permission of Zondervan Bible Publishers.

Illustrations by Corbin Hillam

Library of Congress Cataloging in Publication Data

Speck, Greg.
    Sex: it's worth waiting for / by Greg Speck.
        p. cm.
    Summary: From a Christian perspective, discusses the ethical aspects of such sexual questions as masturbation, pregnancy, premarital sex, and homosexuality.
    ISBN 0-8024-7692-9
    1. Sex instruction for youth—Religious aspects—Christianity.
[1. Sex—Religious aspects—Christianity.   2. Sexual ethics.
3. Christian life.]   I. Title.
HQ35.S624   1989
306.7'07—dc20   89-36571
                                                           CIP
                                                            AC

9 10

Printed in the United States of America

To Bonnie, my friend, lover, and wife.
Other than my Lord, there is no one
I love more. Being married to Bonnie
was worth waiting for.

Special thanks are due the following individuals for their help
with this book. Thank you for your time. Thank you for your
effort. Most of all thank you for your friendship.

Stephen A. Bly	Ralph Gustafson
Dave Busby	Doug Houck
Gary Chapman	Marvin Jacobo
Fritz Dale	Mel Johnson
Joe Donaldson	Marty Larsen
Brian Farka	Kevin Leman
Brian Float	Scott Pederson
Steve French	Julie Peterson
Gail Groenink	Scott Peterson

Dann Spader

And to Tom Ives and Dave Childers, for their hospitality in
London so that I could work on this book.

Contents

1

I Know That!
(Sex Is More Than a Single Act)

Let's be real. We all have questions.☐

Couples have come to me in tears, saying, "Greg, we don't know what happened. We wanted to wait until marriage, but we were just sitting there kissing and touching—and it happened!"

It's like saying, "Something jumped up and bit us."

I had just finished speaking to a group of about 800 teens concerning the whole area of sexual relationships. Hanging around at the back of the crowd was a beautiful tall blonde—bright blue eyes, tan and stylish. She waited till most of the other teens had left. Then she came up and asked if we could talk in private.

We walked over to the side, and she said, "This is really embarrassing, but I need to ask you a question."

She wasn't making eye contact with me, and I could tell she was uncomfortable. But I assured her she could ask any question she wanted to ask and that I'd give her an honest answer.

After taking a deep breath she said, "Well, my boyfriend says that if we have sex standing up then I can't get pregnant. Is that true?"

I felt like crying and laughing at the same time. Here was this beautiful seventeen-year-old being manipulated by her boyfriend because she was basically ignorant about sex.

I told her that what her boyfriend had told her was not true. She could become just as pregnant standing up as lying down. We then had the chance to discuss some other areas she was confused about as well.

Now we're a part of the sexually enlightened generation. We're supposed to know all there is to know about sex. Ask the wrong question in sex education class, and the room erupts in laughter. The guy in front of you turns around and says, "Didn't you know *that?*"

With that kind of pressure, we would rather just sit and smirk and say, "I *know* that!"

But let's be real. We all have questions. We don't know it all. So let me talk with you about two areas basic to the understanding of sex and sexuality: What is sex? and, How does the opposite sex respond?

WHAT IS SEX?

What is sex? Now all of us ought to know the answer to that question, but let me tell you what I usually hear. A couple will come to see me. We will talk, and after a while the guy will say something like this:

Guy: "Greg, we have decided not to have sex until we get married."
Greg: "Great! That's fantastic. But let me ask you a question. What is sex?"
Guy: "Huh?"
Greg: "What is sex?"
Guy: "Don't you know?"
Greg: "Yes, but I want to hear what you think it is."
Guy: "Well ... uh ... it's a ... you see ... we could ... I mean we wouldn't ... not now ... later ... I

mean after . . . after we're married! . . . It's only
. . . because . . . well I . . . Could you repeat the
question, please?"

Greg: "What is sex?"

Guy: "Oh yeah . . . well . . . um . . . you see, sex is intercourse, and we're not going to have intercourse
until we get married! . . . Phew!"

Now what is he saying? He is saying that sex is an
act. And that is absolutely wrong! Sex isn't just an act.
Sex is a progression. Sex begins with kissing. It goes
on to petting, then to heavy petting, and finally has its
climax in intercourse.

The couple that does everything up to intercourse
but stops short of intercourse itself is doing something
unnatural to both bodies.

Here's what happens. You stop the car in this isolated, romantic spot overlooking the dump. Then you
talk for at least thirty to forty seconds. All of a sudden
your lips touch.

You begin to softly kiss, and your body says,
"Oooh, this is nice!"

Then you move to heavy kissing (this has nothing
to do with weight), and your body says, "I think I'm
getting excited!"

You move into petting, and your body says, "I
know I'm excited!"

Then it's heavy petting, and your body says,
"THIS IS BETTER THAN CHOCOLATE CHIP ICE
CREAM!"

All of a sudden you say, "Stop!"

To which your body replies, "AAUGH!"

At that point, what happens between you and
your body?

You feel: Anxiety.

Your body says: "I can't take this kind of abuse anymore. What if I never get a chance to

experience intercourse? What if I die to-morrow? What if she dies tomorrow? What if our parents find out? We'll both die tomorrow!"

You feel: Frustration.
Your body says: "I never have any fun. You've got me on a diet. You make me run every morn-ing. You never change your socks. And now this!"

You feel: Pressure.
Your body says: "You don't understand what this is do-ing to me. I can't take it anymore. You don't get me enough sleep. I can't hear anything because of those headphones. I haven't seen a vegetable in six months. I can't remember my locker combination. And this date isn't turn-ing out the way I wanted it to. I'm warning you—I think I'm going to blow up, or, if not that, at least I'll throw up."

You feel: Anger.
Your body says: "If you ever do this to me again I'll give you hoof-and-mouth disease!"

You see, our bodies were never, ever meant to build to that point and then stop. That's why we feel all those emotions. And usually what those emotions do is to encourage us to put pressure on the other per-son. So we begin to give out some stupid line. Let me give you an example of some common lines and some possible answers:

Line: "If you love me, you'll let me!"
You: "If you love me, you won't."

Line: "I can't believe you said no."
You: "I can't believe that you even asked."

Line: "Don't you love me?"
You: "Don't you respect me?"

Line: "I'll just call someone else."
You: "Here's a quarter."

Line: "It's no big deal."
You: "It's a big deal to God, and it's a big deal to me!"

Line: "But I just want to express my love to you."
You: "The best way to do that is to stop pressuring me."

Line: "I already told everybody that we did it."
You: "Fine, then I don't have to do it a second time."

Line: "I won't tell anyone."
You: "That's because there will be nothing to tell."

Line: "I can't help myself. The pressure is too strong."
You: "Let's go to my house then. I'm sure my family can help you develop some self-control."

Line: "Either we do it now, or we'll break up."
You: " 'Bye."

Line: "You know I could force you if I wanted to."
You: "Either drive me home or to the nearest police station, NOW!" (If need be, leave the car, and call someone to come pick you up.)

Line: "You tell me you love me, but you don't mean it."
You: "Does that mean that you think I'm a liar? If you can't believe what I say, then you can't possibly trust me, because I am my word."

Line: "I've never wanted anyone as much as I want you."

You: "That's wonderful. Let's pray now and ask God to bless this relationship as we continue to follow and glorify Him."

Line: "What's the matter? Are you scared or gay or diseased?"

You: "No, just grossed out! Listen, anytime I choose to I can lose my virginity, and it's sure not going to be to someone who stoops to name calling."

Line: "Nobody is going to care."

You: "OK, let's just go ask my dad."

Line: "But I need to have sex."

You: "Wrong! Sex is a drive that can be controlled. Needs for you would be food, water, oxygen, and a cold shower."

Line: "I'm leaving tomorrow, and who knows when we'll see each other again?"

You: "Wow! Well then, let's be sure and write."

Line: "OK. Let's take off our clothes and just be together. We don't have to touch or anything."

You: "Do I look that stupid to you?"

Line: "Everybody is doing it!"

You: "That's not true. I'm not doing it, and tonight neither are you!" (smile).

Line: "Someday we'll get married. I promise."

You: "And I promise you that it will be worth waiting for."

It's so important that you do not allow others to manipulate and pressure you to give in.

Ladies, there are guys who will say whatever they need to say to get you to take your clothes off. You've got to get a lot tougher. When some guy is pressuring you, you don't have to be kind! Tell him in a straight-forward manner. Don't beat around the bush. If you want a guy to respect you, then you need to demand respect for yourself. You will not get that respect if you allow some guy to put his hands all over your body.

Listen to one woman's experience:

> I was going with a 17-year-old last year for 2 months. I was 15. He broke the relationship off, and I took a lot of things into consideration and came to the conclusion that he dumped me because I would not "make love" with him. He hurt me a lot, and I grieved for quite some time.
>
> A year went by, and he came around again and wanted me to go back with him. Like a stupid fool I went back with him. From the first day we started going out, he told me he loved me every chance he got. I fell head over heels in love with him, and after going together for . . .

How long do you think it took this guy to get this girl to take off her clothes?

> After going together for three days I made love with him. We made love almost every chance we got. I figured by doing this I would keep him. I never did anything to hurt him or get him upset. Everything seemed perfect.
>
> After going together for 2 months, he just up and decided he didn't want to go with me anymore. Well, I am very hurt and feel like all his "I love yous" were a bunch of lies. I have been used, and the hurt has now turned into bitter hate.

Do you think that if this girl had a chance to do it over again she would do things differently? Yes! So don't you make the same stupid mistake. When someone tries to hit on you, remember that you don't have to be kind—be tough!

Now men know there is what is called the aggressive female. Today guys have been laughed at, teased, ridiculed, sworn at, threatened, and gossiped about because they were not aggressive enough sexually on dates. Guys have told me that girls have accused them of being gay because they didn't want to have intercourse.

Some guys get involved sexually not because they want to but because they have been pressured by the girl.

Men, how do we deal with this situation? The answers are not easy, but let me suggest some things you need to be aware of.

☐ Don't date a woman who has a reputation for aggressiveness and sleeping around.

Imagine being on a date where the woman takes off her clothes and attempts to undress you! You don't need to be strong to withstand that sort of temptation —you need to be comatose!

☐ Date only women who are Christians.

Now this doesn't necessarily solve the problem. Some women who claim to be Christians are sexually active. However, if you are careful to date a godly woman, you won't have to worry.

☐ But let's say you go out with this woman, and you didn't realize what kind of reputation she has.

You've been studying so hard you haven't had time to even think about women (sure!). But you're on the date, and suddenly this woman begins to hit on you. What do you do?

First, try to understand her. This is a pattern she has fallen into. It is something she has learned men like. She may feel this sort of behavior is expected of her on a date. Besides, it's a fast and easy way for her to feel close to someone else.

But let's also understand that this woman needs help. Someone must help her break the pattern. The longer she continues, the harder she will become and the more problems she will cause for herself.

What can you do to help her?

Why not be radical? Why not say, "Wait a second! I like you, you're great looking, but I want to get to know you as a person." You see, quite a few guys know this woman's body, but you are saying, "I want to know you as someone, not as just a body."

What if she laughs? She probably will, because she is so shocked. But deep down she is looking for a man who will respect and care about her.

So you can use her and be one in a line of guys, or you can care about her and make an impression she won't forget. I'm betting she is looking for a guy who is willing to try to understand her. Even if she doesn't respond positively, believe me, when she matures she will look back and realize that you were one of those few who really cared about her. That's what you want to be remembered for—not as one in a long line of lovers. You have the opportunity to give her hope.

☐ Don't isolate yourself.

Chances are she's not going to attack you in a public place like Denny's. Don't put yourself in a spot where she has the chance to become aggressive.

☐ Think about the Lord.

He is right there, watching you. Pray to Him silently. Ask the Holy Spirit to give you special courage and wisdom, the right words to say and the right actions to take.

☐ Remember that an aggressive woman can't make you become involved sexually.

You can be a man of character. If she starts undressing in the car, then drive to a lighted public area. She will put her clothes back on. If you're at a party, then leave.

Now, I realize that there are guys who have been raped by women. This can happen when the woman is much bigger physically, the guy is drunk or high on drugs, or there is a group of women. Again it's important that you do not isolate yourself.

☐ So what happens if the woman later says terrible things about you? You're "gay, scared, less than a man," and so on.

I guess my response is, "So what?" Your friends are your friends. They aren't going to believe her. Your enemies don't like you anyway, whether you went to bed with her or not. And other people aren't as dumb as you may think. They know the woman's reputation, and they know who is more likely to be telling the truth. Plus, believe it or not, most people could care less what went on between you.

If people ask, "How come you didn't sleep with her?" you can say, "Because I didn't want to. Because I think I'm worth more than a one-night stand. Because I don't want to be manipulated into having sex with anyone. And it's pretty egotistical on her part to think that if a man doesn't want intercourse with her then he must be gay."

You'll find a lot of individuals agreeing with you, and you will gain respect in the eyes of many. There is a whole group of women who will be very attracted to a man with that kind of character. This will open the door for you to tell them the most important reason you didn't get involved—because you love Jesus so much!

For you who are reading this and are sexually involved right now, do you want to find out if this person really loves you or not? Try this. Go to him or her and say, "I love you so much and think you are so special. But I want us to work on other areas of our relationship, so I want to stop the sex."

You'll discover fast whether the person loves you. Some of you know right now what would happen if you said that. Your "friend" would be out the door. Now if you know that and continue to be involved with the guy or girl sexually, you're not somebody—you're something!

If you want respect, then demand it! If someone tries to touch you where you don't want to be touched, say, "This is my body. This is not your body. Get your hands off my body!"

Talk with your parents. Make a deal that if you ever are in a situation where you are being pressured, you can call them and they will come and get you no matter where you are or what time it is.

So, number one, remember that sex is a progression. When we move into the heavy petting stage, one of four things usually occurs:

☐ You end up having intercourse.
☐ Because of all the pressure and problems that result, you break up.
☐ You get married just in time.
☐ By God's grace you are able to pull back on your physical affection and set new standards.

Don't start the progression, and you won't have to worry about where it's all going to end.

HOW DOES THE OPPOSITE SEX RESPOND?

How does the opposite sex respond? Ladies, do you understand how males respond, and, gentlemen, do you understand about women?

Researchers brought a group of men into a room. They wired up whatever needed to be wired up to measure their emotional responses and then began to flash pictures upon a screen. They flashed the picture of a . . .

Flower. Yawn. Not much reaction.
Hot car. Mmm. The needle began to move.
Baby. Oops. No baby. Very little needle movement.
Naked woman. Wow! All of a sudden there were lights, bells, and buzzers. The needle moved off the page!

Ladies, you need to understand that a man, generally speaking, is visually oriented. That means that by just looking at you he can become sexually excited. He doesn't even have to touch you.

Now some women say to me, "Oh, come on, I don't believe that. That's stupid."

If you women would walk down to a gas station or quick-shop market, you would see a section of maga-

zines called "pornographic." Now if you picked up these magazines—and I highly recommend you don't do this—you would discover that all of them have one thing in common. They are filled with pictures of naked women.

Now why do you think pornographic magazines and videos are such big sellers? Because a man can buy or rent one, and by looking at the pictures he can become sexually excited.

Matthew 5:28 tells me that if I look lustfully at a woman, that is wrong. But, ladies, you can do a lot to help me and the rest of the brothers not to lust. How? By what you wear!

For example, what does your swimsuit look like? If your suit is somewhat revealing—and you know better than anyone else if it's revealing—when you are around the water what do you think the guys are looking at? If you think it's your pretty little eyes, then you are wrong. In many cases they are checking out your body and lusting after you.

Women have said to me, "Oh, I just love it when guys lust after me. It's so exciting!"

If that's your reaction, then you don't understand what goes on in the mind of a man. When a man lusts after you, you become a piece of meat! He could care less that you have hopes, needs, dreams, and desires. All he wants to do is get his hands on your body. *Lusting* is not a complimentary term.

Women, I know some guys would lust after you if you wore a bathing suit with long sleeves, pant legs, and a turtleneck. That's not your fault. That's the fault of the guys. What I am saying is, look good, be stylish, but don't compromise yourself as a woman.

Stay away from tight jeans, dresses slit up the side, short skirts, halter tops, low-cut tops, sleeveless sweaters with big underarms, and running around bra-less. Listen to your mother when it comes to the question, Is this sensual or not? Dad also ought to be able to give you some insights.

Put on your outfit, stand at the mirror, and ask yourself, "What am I trying to draw attention to?" If it's just to your exterior, then in many cases you're going to be treated like a piece of meat. Doesn't it make sense that, if you seek to emphasize certain parts of your body, then you will attract men who are primarily interested in those parts of your body?

Guys, there is something that really bugs women. When you talk with a woman it's important that you make eye contact with her. Stop staring at her chest. You don't think she notices, but she does.

Again, males tend to be visually oriented. And again I am speaking in generalities. You could say, "Well, that isn't true of my Uncle Harry!" OK, bless

Uncle Harry's heart. Maybe it isn't, but generally the statement is true.

Understand also that the male usually reaches his sexual peak—when the sexual drive is strongest—somewhere between the ages of sixteen and twenty-five. But in most cases a woman does not reach her sexual peak until between twenty-five and forty-five. For that reason there may be a big difference in the way they react. For the woman, the sexual drive may not be strong, but for the guy it may be powerful. If you are not aware of these basics, you may find yourself in trouble.

And stay away from alcohol. Drinking can free up a person so that he or she is more easily seduced. When you've been drinking, it's much easier for someone to talk you into taking off your clothes.

Now what about those researchers and the women? They wired up the women and began to show them pictures of a . . .

Flower. Nice. Needle moved a little.
Hot car. Huh? Not much movement.
Naked man. Hardly any movement. What a blow to the male ego!

Do you know what got the biggest reaction from the women? The cute little cuddly baby. (This is a little off the subject, but one guy came to me after I shared this and said, "Boy, from now on I'm carrying around baby pictures." Obviously he got a lot out of my talk.)

The woman, generally speaking, is touch oriented. It is usually not until the petting stage, when her body is being caressed, that she gets turned on.

That's why people have put pressure on the women and have said, "Ladies, it's your responsibility to handle the physical part of the relationship. If things get carried away, it's your fault." Now I say garbage to that! Men, we need to take responsibility in that area and seek to love the woman, which means not to use or abuse her.

But the reason men have said this to you ladies is this. If you allow the relationship to get to the petting stage and lose control emotionally, chances are that the guy's lost control a mile down the road. If you don't say no, then he won't say no, and you end up having intercourse.

So understand these two basics—(1) sex is a progression, and (2) men and women respond differently. Apply them to your dating relationships, and you will be saved a lot of hassle.

How Far Can I Go?
(Intercourse, Petting, Kissing)

"We really love each other and have been dating for a long time and I want to know how far we can go." ☐

Recently I spoke at a Christian high school's spiritual emphasis week. They had an optional meeting one night, when the students could write down any questions they wanted to ask me.

Now not everyone turned in a question (couldn't think of one, couldn't write, were in a coma, etc.) But of the fifty or so questions I received, at least twelve asked this kind of question: "We really love each other and have been dating for a long time [at least two weeks] and I want to know how far we can go."

That's the big question I am always getting. I think by asking that question we are saying, "I'm curious, plus it feels good, so I want to go as far as I can while still being a Christian." It's natural to be curious, and curiosity ought to raise questions. Ask them! We ought to be able to deal with sex in a straightforward manner within the Body of Christ.

You're also right. It does feel good. It should. God made it! But the question you ask is bad. Most of us want to know how far we can push it—how close we can get to the fire without actually getting burned.

If sex is so great (and it is!)—if sex is so wonderful (and it is!)—if sex is so exciting (and it is!)—then I shouldn't be asking how close I can get to destroying that good thing. I should be asking, rather, how far away should I stay so that I can eventually experience God's very best.

What if I took you and your friends with me to Switzerland for an all-expense-paid vacation? What if I took you up the Jungfräu where there was a sheer drop of several thousand feet? How many would ask, "Oh boy, how close can I get?" Would you run to the edge and hang your toes over? "Oh boy, look at me . . . oops! Stop pushing. Oh no . . . ahhh . . . !" *Splat!*

No, that would be stupid. We know what would happen. As they say, "The fall never kills you—it's that sudden stop at the bottom."

But some of us are trying to get as close as we can to the edge sexually. We want to see how physical we can get, and we're about to take a major fall.

So what are some guidelines? Ephesians 5:3 says there shouldn't even be a "hint of sexual immorality." God isn't even talking about your actually being involved sexually. He just says there shouldn't be the slightest hint.

That is to say, what you do in public suggests what you must do in private. People are going to jump to that conclusion whether you're sexually involved or not. So don't give them any cause to think of that at all.

Men, we should always seek to protect the reputation of the woman we are with. We don't want anyone to think less of a woman because she is out with us.

You've seen the couple at your school who make out between classes. We look at that, and there is the tendency to think, *If they do this in the hallway, what must they do in private?* What this does is to cheapen the guy or girl in the eyes of other people. So in your relationship there shouldn't be even a hint of sexual immorality.

How far can I go? If you want some thoughts, here they are:

WHAT ABOUT INTERCOURSE?

What about premarital intercourse? God says it's wrong. No rationalizing will change that fact. You can make a lot of excuses, but never ever say that God approves. He doesn't. Fornication is a premarital sexual relationship, and God tells us not to do that. 1 Thessalonians 4:3 says, "It is God's will that you should be sanctified [set apart for God's use]; that you should avoid sexual immorality."

Individuals have said to me, "It's OK because we really love each other." They are saying that love makes premarital sex OK and cancels God's command against it.

"It's OK because it feels so right." But feelings do not tend to be a good indicator of the difference between right and wrong. It might also feel right to lie, shoplift, gossip, rape, murder, or disobey your parents. If you could eliminate one of God's commands because you *felt* a certain way, you could eliminate them all. There would then be no clear moral standard of right and wrong.

Remember also that your personal happiness is not the most important concern. The most important concern when you date should be God and others! We exercise discipline over ourselves and our relationships. We ask ourselves the question, What is best for the person I'm dating? How can I help this person develop?

WHAT ABOUT PETTING?

What is petting? It's the fondling, caressing, of each other's body, especially the breasts and genitals. In marriage we would call this foreplay, because it prepares for intercourse by getting one another sexually excited.

I have heard this great excuse for petting: "We want to wait until we get married to have intercourse, so we pet because it releases our sexual tension, thus protecting our virginity."

Now that sounds pretty good at face value. But when you look closer you discover that it's a terrible excuse. Why? Because petting does not build up tolerance against further desire; it does just the opposite. It sexually excites you and reduces your self-control.

It is dumb for a couple to rationalize that because engaging in intercourse is a temptation to them, their best protection is to pet. By petting they are only drawing closer and closer to intercourse. Petting was not designed to satisfy but to excite!

Remember that petting is subject to the moral law of diminishing returns. That means the more you do something the less exciting it is. So in order to keep petting exciting, and to gain satisfaction, the amount and intensity of the petting must continue to increase. The problem is that petting without a climax cannot be increased in intensity indefinitely.

So the person involved in petting usually goes through four stages:

1. This is great! I feel so close to you. The more I'm involved the more exciting it is, and I just want to be with you all the time.
2. I've seen everything there is to see. I've touched everything there is to touch, and I'm getting kind of bored. The more I get, the less the satisfaction.
3. The satisfaction isn't even worth the effort. We both feel used, and petting becomes crude, old, and disgusting.
4. We break up, usually finding another partner and starting this pattern all over again.

How do we keep getting into this mess over and over again?

Well, we are really attracted to one another. Sometimes we even call it love. We go out together, but the date is unplanned, and we have a lot of time on our hands. We rationalize that petting is a way of expressing our love to each other. Besides, it feels good!

It relieves the boredom, requires no intelligence, and is no challenge to the personality.

But more and more, petting begins to control us. We want to go further and further. First we touch each other. Then our hands go under the clothes. Then the clothes come off, and there we are—two naked bodies seeking to satisfy our own desires, rather than caring for the other person.

Soon all our relationships begin to deteriorate. We ignore our friends and families. Our relationship with God goes right down the tubes. And instead of going out on a date to get to know each other, we are stuck in the same old rut, two people sharing their least common denominator, their bodies.

The well-known Kinsey report on sex and sexual behavior says this: "Petting which does not proceed to a climax may seriously disturb a person, possibly leaving one or both individuals in a state of nervous tension, a tension that may produce hypersensitivity and an increased irritability, all of which in time will strain the relationship of the couple and possibly prevent the development of love and the desire for marriage."

Dr. Kinsey is saying that it is better to pet to a climax or not to pet at all. But as Christians we must face the fact that petting to a climax is morally little different from intercourse itself.

What is done is usually either to mutually masturbate one another or to perform oral sex. A girl said to me, "Well, at least I'm still a virgin!" My answer: "You may be a virgin physically, but you certainly aren't one experientially."

However, if we don't pet to a climax we can add psychological problems to our relationship. Plus remember Ephesians 5:3? I believe that petting certainly hints of sexual immorality. As a matter of fact I don't think it hints of it; I think it screams of it.

So what do we do? It is obvious that petting ought not be a part of a Christian's dating relationships. Now you who have been to the petting stage and beyond may find my position impossible. But don't give up. Check out chapter 13.

WHAT ABOUT KISSING?

Well then, what about kissing? What about "making out" for an hour and a half until our lips bleed?

Kissing ought to be a giving experience. "Because I love you I want to give you this kiss." But let's face it, for all of us who have made out it wasn't a giving experience. It became a taking experience. This is unhealthy, because you begin to want to go further by unbuttoning, unzipping, unsnapping, untying, un-Velcroing, ungluing, unbolting—unbelievable! Sex is progressive, remember, and once you get started it is hard to stop.

Kissing that takes becomes unhealthy for the other person, because we begin to use him or her to satisfy our own desires.

Your kisses ought to be valuable. You shouldn't just hand them out like handshakes, because if you really end up liking the person, what are you going to give next—a kiss? No, you've already given that, and now you are farther down the road than you really ought to be.

People ask me, "Are you saying that kissing is a sin? Then I've sinned millions of times!" No, I am not saying that kissing is a sin, but where does the Bible say that to have a healthy relationship you must be involved physically? Nowhere. As a matter of fact,

some of the unhealthiest relationships I've known of are ones that were physical.

After you have been dating for a while, I see nothing wrong with a good-night kiss, or a kiss of appreciation, or a kiss to say "You're really special." But remember, ladies, you don't owe any guy a kiss. Maybe a guy says to you, "Hey, I took you out to a nice place to eat. Didn't you enjoy Burger King? You owe me a kiss!"

You say to him, "I don't owe you a kiss because you had the pleasure of taking me out." If he doesn't take you out anymore because you wouldn't kiss him, then he really doesn't like you. He is just attracted to your luscious lips.

It's important that you set or reestablish your standards now! If you wait until the car stops on this dark road to decide what you will and will not do, it's too late. What should your standard be? Well, let me ask you this, "What turns you on?" Now take a giant step back from there, and be tough on yourself!

The world ought to see a difference in the relationships of Christians. We need to stand out as lights, without a hint of immorality, in a darkening world. "You are the light of the world. . . . Let your light shine before men, that they may see your good deeds and praise your Father in heaven" (Matthew 5:14, 16).

Our standards should be so high that the world and our friends notice a distinct difference. Then when they question us, we can tell them about Jesus Christ and how He has made a difference in our lives.

Talk with your parents. Ask them about their sexual involvement before marriage. Do they have any regrets? What would they have done differently? If they dated now, what would their standards be? Were they insecure? How did they get out of a potentially sexual situation? But no matter what their answer, the bottom line is that you are seeking to glorify Jesus Christ.

I know it won't be easy, but be tough and wait. It's worth waiting for.

What Does God Have to Do with Sex?
(The Positives of Sexuality)

It's time we look at sex and sexual relationships from God's point of view. □

I want to start out by saying that sex is great. It's wonderful, tremendous, exciting, spectacular, and awesome! And sex has a lot to do with God because He is the one who made it.

God made Adam and Eve "male and female" (Genesis 1:27-31 and 2:25). He made them sexual beings, and they stood before Him naked. What was God's reaction to them? Did He say . . .

"Gross Me out—put something on! Here, take this Lee Rider leaf!"

No.

Or, "Well, I guess it'll have to do."

No.

Or even, "It's good."

No, God looked at them and said, "They are very good!"

You are a sexual being, and sex is very good. There is nothing gross, dirty, or terrible about it.

It's time we look at sex and sexual relationships from God's point of view.

God is not against sex. That should be obvious, since He is the one who made it. Since He made it, it would seem reasonable to assume that He ought to know how we can experience sex at its very best.

Madison Avenue and the media have given us a perverted outlook on sex that has really cheapened it. Where did you learn about sex? Here is where teenagers receive their information:

- ☐ 1% credit their parents.
- ☐ 9% say that sex education classes at school were helpful.
- ☐ 90% say their sex information came from peers, TV, movies, music videos, and pornographic magazines! (Josh McDowell stated in *Group* magazine, Feb. 1985, that the average American will see 9,230 acts or implied acts of sex on TV a year.)

Brent Miller, Utah State University sociologist, in a study of 1,150 teenagers shows that teens are less likely to be sexually active if they participate in family events and if they learn the facts from their parents instead from friends.

Because we are so bombarded by sex we tend to lose our perspective. What is the purpose of sex?

Sex Is God's Creation

Sex is wonderful, but I want you to know that sex must be held in proper perspective—that is, within a marriage relationship where male and female have first committed themselves to one another spiritually, emotionally, and intellectually. When we take sex out of the proper place God has created it for and put it in the backseat of a car, or at a party when the parents are gone, it begins to become "gross" and "dirty," but God never planned it that way.

A young woman once told me, "Greg, I have a boy-friend, and I want you to know that we are having intercourse. Do you know what I do first thing after coming home from a date? I take a shower, because I feel so dirty that I want to wash it all away!"

How sad. God never meant us to experience guilt after sexual relationships. But this is what happens when we compromise God's plan for our lives.

Again, God is not against sex. He created it. He wants us to enjoy this wonderful gift. We do not stay away from premarital sex because something is wrong with sex. We stay away from premarital sex because

☐ It keeps us from God's best.
☐ In the long run it will cause far more emotional and spiritual pain than it will ever give physical pleasure.
☐ It's contrary to God's purpose for our lives.

We experience sex at its ultimate when we participate in it the way God intended, and that is within a marriage relationship.

"But I want to be free! What has happened to freedom?"

If you are a Christian, you are free. Look at John 8:36—"If the Son sets you free, you will be free indeed."

"Yeah, well then, how come I'm limited and can't have sex right now?"

It's important we realize that there are limitations in all of God's creation. For example, take a cute little sparrow. Isn't it a shame that this bird is limited to sky and land only? Three-fourths of the earth's surface is covered by water. It isn't fair—this sparrow should be able to go under water.

So we take the sparrow down to sixty feet, where all the beautiful coral formations are, and we set it free.

"Swim, little sparrow, swim!—you're not swimming. As a matter of fact, you're not even moving! Uh-oh."

Or take a big, beautiful rainbow trout. It's not fair that this fish should be limited to the water. There is so much to do and see on land. So we take the trout to downtown Chicago, and we let it go.

"Now you can check out the John Hancock Building, do some shopping at Water Tower Place, and visit the famous Moody Bible Institute—come on, all you're doing is flopping around. You can buy a great underwater watch. What's wrong? Maybe you want something to eat. This place has a great fish fry with—oops, I mean how about pizza? How come you don't want to

eat? How come you don't want to buy anything? How come you don't want to see anything? How come you've stopped flopping around?"

Finally take a kitten, this tiny fur ball. Would you say, "It isn't fair that this kitten be limited to the ground—it should have the opportunity to fly!"?

So we take the kitten to the top of the Sears Tower and throw it off. "You're free! Fly, fly, fly—hm, it just missed the trout."

This was not freedom for the sparrow, the trout, or the kitten because their freedom is found within the limitations of what God has created them to be and to become.

We are free to be all that God has created us to be, but there are limitations. I hope it has become obvious to you that God's limitations are not to stifle you but are there for your good.

Yes, we're free within limitations, and you will discover that these limitations will actually heighten your joy and truly give you life that satisfies. God desires what is best for us.

Sin will manipulate, bind, control, and eventually kill you. Jesus Christ wants to set you free. He wants you to experience life that will last forever. Romans 6:23 says, "The wages of sin is death, but the gift of God is eternal life in Christ Jesus our Lord."

Freedom will never be found in doing something contrary to the very purpose for which God created the human body. "The body is not meant for sexual immorality, but for the Lord, and the Lord for the body" (1 Corinthians 6:13). The body is not meant for premarital sex. And God ought to know, because He created sex.

SEX IS WONDERFUL IN A MARRIAGE RELATIONSHIP

"May your fountain be blessed, and may you rejoice in the wife of your youth. A loving doe, a graceful deer—may her breasts satisfy you always, may you ever be captivated by her love" (Proverbs 5:18-19.)

Sex has always been wonderful, and the place to enjoy it is in a marriage relationship. The sexual relationship with your husband or wife is a time for rejoicing, laughter, encouragement, enjoyment, and becoming one.

First Corinthians 7:9 indicates that there are many men and women who have a deep desire for sexual relationships: "If they cannot control themselves, they should marry, for it is better to marry than to burn with passion." Marriage gives us an opportunity to fulfill those desires, free of guilt, in a way that is pleasing and honoring to God.

SEX MAKES YOU ONE WITH THAT OTHER PERSON

Sexual relationships are so important that in Genesis 2:24 God sets out some specific steps that are to be taken: "For this reason a man will leave his father and mother and be united to his wife, and they will become one flesh."

We are first to leave and then to be united. The result of that leaving and uniting is becoming "one flesh."

These steps are so important that Jesus Christ puts His stamp of approval on them in Matthew 19:5-6 and Mark 10:7-9.

Let's look at the two steps and their result in more detail.

LEAVE

Simply stated, this means to become married. You are leaving your home and your parents to begin a new life with another individual.

Marriage is a huge step and one that is taken much too lightly. Today it's not unusual to live to be seventy. If you marry at twenty, then you are saying that you will live with this other person for more than fifty years. That is twice as long as you have already lived.

The decision to marry is one that should not be made on the basis of our emotions. It's a commitment you make to that other person "till death do you part." God remains your #1 priority, but your #2 priority becomes your spouse. Divorce is not an option. That is why it is so important that you are sure, and your parents and godly friends are supportive, before you take this step.

People say to me, "What's the big deal about getting married and signing a piece of paper? Is it that important?" Yes, for two reasons.

1. It was God who ordained marriage, and you are being obedient to Him. We set ourselves up for a lot of pain when we try to skirt what God has already established as good and right. Obviously you can't expect God to bless if you have disobeyed Him.
2. You are publicly declaring the deep love and commitment you have for one another. You are vowing to love that person "for richer, for poorer, in sickness and in health, for better or for worse." And, believe me, there will be some worse.

If you really love and are committed to each other, there is no reason you wouldn't want to be publicly married. If you're not ready to take that step, then you aren't ready for sex. Sex at its very ultimate, the way God intended it, is found only in a relationship of total commitment—marriage.

Women have said to me, "My boyfriend is afraid of marriage because of all the pain and problems it can cause. We love each other, and he says he wants to save me from that pain, so he thinks we should live together. What do you think?"

My response to that is "Don't be stupid! When you live with him you are giving him all the benefits of a marriage relationship without any of the responsibilities." Anytime he wants to he can walk out the door, and in many cases he does.

Listen, there will be some pain and hard times because that is a part of love, marriage, commitment.

UNITE

How do we become united? We are united by our mutual commitment, made visible through the marriage ceremony, and by the unseen union God creates. One aspect of this union is sexual intercourse. This uniting is meant to form a lasting relationship that is to be broken only by death.

For example, take two pieces of paper and glue them together. Let them sit for twenty-four hours, and then attempt to separate them. Try as you might, all you end up doing is tearing, ripping, and destroying the paper. The pieces have become inseparable.

The same is true in a relationship where there has been intercourse. To separate will cause tremendous pain, problems, and destruction.

You are never, ever meant to part from the person you have had intercourse with. The sex relationship is not supposed to be a cheap thrill but rather the uniting of two individuals within the boundaries of marriage.

Too many teenagers have turned these steps around. Instead of leaving and uniting, they are uniting and then leaving.

ONE FLESH

Here is the result of doing it God's way. You leave, you unite, and then in God's eyes you are "one flesh." To become that close to another human being is wonderful. Now the problem is that even if you don't take God's steps, and you sleep together at a party on Friday night, you still become one flesh. But this is not the wonderful, beautiful plan God had for you. Casual sex degrades God's gift.

It's like being presented as a gift the magnificent Michaelangelo sculpture *David*, then taking this perfect gift and hitting it with a hammer. You have abused it, and it will never be the same again. Some of us seek after cheap thrills and think they have no lasting impact on our lives. But they do.

For this reason, it is so very important that we stay away from prostitutes. (Look at Proverbs 9:13-18; 23:27-28.)

☐ Our bodies are a part of Christ's Body.

When you have intercourse with a prostitute you are joining Christ's Body with a whore. God commands us not to do that. "Do you not know that your bodies are members of Christ himself? Shall I then take the members of Christ and unite them with a prostitute? Never!" (1 Corinthians 6:15).

☐ Think also of all the possibilities of disease.

Who knows who or what a prostitute has slept with? Your chances of catching all kinds of sexually transmitted diseases are greatly increased. Don't do it! It's not worth it!

☐ Remember that intercourse causes you to be "one flesh."

Even if you feel no commitment or love, you still become one flesh, because the sex relationship is that important. You can try to keep the act casual, but it just isn't casual.

☐ Having sex with you is for a prostitute like going grocery shopping.

It's commonplace, something she does all the time. There is no love, no joy, no excitement on her part. She isn't becoming turned on. She is merely an actress playing a part. She is a liar and will say whatever she needs to say to get your money. She isn't attracted to you; she is merely using you.

☐ You never, ever forget.

Yes, you can be forgiven, but the memories linger, causing you guilt, sorrow, and self-hate.

☐ Think of all the good you might do with the money it costs you for this momentary pleasure that never really satisfies.

☐ This prostitute needs help desperately.

She is someone, someone's daughter, someone with needs, hurts, dreams, and hopes. Under that tough outside beats a heart like the rest of us have. Instead of trying to help, you merely add to her hurt.

SEX AS GOD INTENDED IT IS A GIVING EXPERIENCE

"The husband should fulfill his marital duty to his wife, and likewise the wife to her husband. The wife's body does not belong to her alone but also to her husband. In the same way the husband's body does not belong to him alone but also to his wife. Do not deprive each other except by mutual consent and for a time, so that you may devote yourselves to prayer. Then come together again so that Satan will not tempt you because of your lack of self control"(1 Corinthians 7:3-5).

In the marriage relationship my desire is to please my wife sexually and to give her satisfaction. I want what is best for her. The same is true of my wife; she wants to please me. So in a marriage relationship we have two individuals who are seeking to give to and please the other person.

In a dating relationship we are usually seeking self-gratification. We want to feel good. We want to be excited. We want all we can get, so we pressure the other person. We are seeking to please ourselves.

Do you love the person you are dating? Let me ask you three questions:

1. Is the relationship morally pure?
2. Because the other person has dated you, does he/she have a better self-image?
3. Because of going out with you, is the other person closer to Christ?

If the answer is yes, then you are probably loving your date. If the answer is no, then you have been lusting.

Sex Is a Wonderful Way to Get to Know Your Husband or Wife

Go through the Bible and notice all the times that the word *know* is substituted for sexual intercourse.

Sex causes you to be vulnerable. You see, before marriage you need to become open—naked—with that other person emotionally, intellectually, and spiritually. The better he or she gets to know you, the more vulnerable you become. Then the final step is the honeymoon, when you become naked and vulnerable before your partner physically.

The sexual relationship in marriage is a great way to keep open the lines of communication. Sex is meant to develop oneness, a wonderful closeness, the desire to be open and vulnerable emotionally.

I am sure that you know a lot of different people in a lot of different ways and at many different levels. But this is one kind of knowing that is special, meant for just you and your spouse.

Remember that though sex is sharing, it is just a part of what is shared in marriage. You also share bills, tears, the flu, laughter, cooking, cleaning, shopping, dirty diapers, praying, worshiping, and reaching out to others. These things are all part of the total commitment you make to each other.

Sex truly becomes better and better and better in a marriage relationship. That is because you are growing together spiritually, emotionally, and intellectually and you are communicating more. You are becoming best friends. Seek to please your spouse in creative and loving ways. Continue to communicate openly and honestly. It makes sense that the longer you are together the better you get to know each other. You become more aware of each other's needs and desires. You learn what best pleases the other person.

What a great way to get to know someone!

SEX IS FUN

Proverbs 5:18 says, "May your fountain be blessed, and may you rejoice in the wife of your youth." Sexual involvement with one's spouse is something to look forward to, something fun to do. Being involved sexually the way God planned is a happy, wonderful experience. But then it ought to be. God, who created the whole universe, also made sex.

What a great gift. Save it. Experience the joy and the fun. Please don't settle for any cheap imitation of God's best.

SEX ENJOYED THE RIGHT WAY IS PLEASING TO GOD

First Timothy 6:17 says, "Command those who are rich in this present world not to be arrogant nor to put their hope in wealth, which is so uncertain, but to put their hope in God, who richly provides us with everything for our enjoyment."

Suppose you buy a child what you consider the perfect Christmas present. If the child opens it, gives a shout of glee, tells you, "Thanks a lot," and begins to play with it, are you upset?

Do you say, "Stop playing with that toy. You come sit here next to me and stop enjoying yourself!" Of course not. You are pleased the child is enjoying the good gift that you brought him.

As a matter of fact you would be pretty upset if he didn't enjoy and use this toy.

Now God has given us sex as a wonderful gift. And when we enjoy the sexual relationship with our spouse in a loving, tender, and giving way, this is pleasing to Him.

We honor and please God by having healthy, exciting sexual relationships within marriage.

SEX IS FOR REPRODUCTION

"God blessed them and said to them, 'Be fruitful and increase in number' "(Genesis 1:28).

To have children is a reason to be involved sexually. Children are an awesome responsibility, but they are truly a blessing from God.

God could have tied reproduction into sticking each other with sharp pins. (If this were the case, we wouldn't have a lot of premarital pin sticking going on.) But our God in His great wisdom linked together the possibility of having children with something as exciting and beautiful as sex!

SEX IS WORTH WAITING FOR (I GUARANTEE IT)

If you decide to wait—and I really hope you do —when you get married give me the telephone number of where you'll be the first night. Next morning, not too early, I'll call you and ask, "Are you glad you waited?" I just know you'll say, "Whoopee, I'm so glad I waited!"

Understand that sexual urges and desires are a part of you. God made you a sexual being, and this creates a struggle within. There is the desire to have sex while knowing you need to wait.

So why didn't God just make me so I wouldn't want premarital sex? Because if He did that you would no longer be a sexual being and you wouldn't want sex within marriage either. Also, to do that would take away your ability to choose. You would merely be a kind of robot programmed to do what God wants. In addition, as you grow He wants to build your character. He wants you to develop and make right choices now so that He can trust you to make right choices later. If you want God to use you in great ways later on, then be faithful in the little areas now.

Our question shouldn't be, "OK, what do I have to do?" but rather, "How much do I love Jesus?" If I truly love someone then I want to please him, and doing that isn't a burden but rather a pleasure.

"But it's so hard!"

That's true, but then nothing of value is ever easy. We develop ourselves not by merely going with the flow and doing what feels good, but by doing what is right whether we feel like it or not. Too often when we need to make a choice, we don't ask ourselves, "Now let's see, is this good for me? Will it develop me? Am I going to profit from it?" Instead we ask, "Will it feel good?" If the answer is yes, then we do it.

But not everything that feels good is good for you. And some of the things that feel the best to you right now can in the long run do tremendous damage. A prime example of that is sex.

Nobody sets out to make mistakes, but it happens, many times because of bad choices based on how good we thought we would feel. God never called you to feel a certain way; He called you to be obedient whether you feel like obeying or not.

Let's understand something else. Sex is not a need! Food is a need. I need food, or I'll starve to death. Water is a need. I need water, or I'll perish. Sex is a need? I need sex, or I'll blow up. *Wrong!* Sex is not a need; it is a drive, and it requires directing. Sex is a powerful drive, and it needs to be controlled.

Sexuality is a deep part of who you are, and it is normal to feel curious. I mean, if you've never been turned on by a member of the opposite sex, then you'd better check the obituaries, because I think you're dead. No matter how spiritual we may be, we will be tempted by the lust of the flesh at one time or another.

It's part of living to feel sexually stimulated and at the same time to control one's desires. We need to learn to live with unfulfilled desires. Don't condemn yourself because you are tempted. Be upset when you yield to the temptation.

Master your body. Don't let your body master you. "It is God's will that you should be sanctified: that you should avoid sexual immorality; that each of you should learn to control his own body in a way that is holy and honorable, not in passionate lust like the heathen who do not know God" (1 Thessalonians 4:3-5).

Your body doesn't even belong to you. You were bought and paid for by Christ on the cross. "Do you not know that your body is a temple of the Holy Spirit, who is in you, whom you have received from God? You are not your own; you were bought at a price. Therefore honor God with your body" (1 Corinthians 6:19-20).

Sex can be compared to a fire. Build a fire in the fireplace on a cold winter evening, and it becomes warm, cozy, inviting, and romantic. But build the fire in your lap, and suddenly it becomes frightening, destructive, and painful.

Sex within the boundaries God has set is wonderful. Take sex beyond those loving boundaries, and it becomes destructive and emotionally very painful.

"Can a man scoop fire into his lap without his clothes being burned?" Proverbs 6:27-29 says. "Can a man walk on hot coals without his feet being scorched? So is he who sleeps with another man's wife; no one who touches her will go unpunished."

I can't make you do what's right. You've got to decide. You've got to purpose in your heart to be strong, courageous, and morally pure.

But remember, ultimate victory will not occur because you follow all the steps Greg Speck lays out in

this book. Your dependency must be upon the Holy Spirit. He is the one who will give you strength, courage, and wisdom to do what is right, even when it's hard.

God says, "Wait, and I'll provide you with the very best. It's worth waiting for." Believe Him. He knows what He is talking about.

4

Reasons for Waiting
(Besides What the Bible Says)

I believe that teenagers today, empowered by the Holy Spirit, can do whatever they set their minds to. □

Have you noticed that many sex education courses, sex "experts," Planned Parenthood, and so on, stress making wise decisions as to *when* you are emotionally ready for sex?

They take the approach that says, "They are going to be sexually involved anyway, so let's at least try to stop unwanted babies either before or after conception." But the answer is not birth control, and it's not abortion. You and I both know that.

Why do people assume that teenagers will not respond to a positive approach that says self-discipline is what we want to strive for?

I believe that teenagers today, empowered by the Holy Spirit, can do whatever they set their minds to. They can turn the tide by saying, "Sex is so great that it's worth waiting for." The turnabout can start with you.

I speak in quite a few public high school assemblies. Obviously I can't talk about God, Christianity, and the Bible there, but still students want to know, Why shouldn't I get involved sexually?

OK, here are some reasons—apart from what the Bible says—for not getting involved sexually.

YOU WANT TO GIVE YOUR BEST

Someday you will probably get married. Now if I asked, "Are you going to love the person you marry?" you would say, "What a stupid question. Sure, I'll love them." You'd probably say you'll love that person more than you've ever loved anyone before.

Then I would ask, "Do you want to give them your very best?" And you would say, "Of course!" I would say, "Great. Then how come we do that in every area but the sexual?"

As women we mess around with Bob, Jim, and Jack, and there is our husband at the bottom of the list. As men, we play around with Sue, Cathy, and Mary, and there's our wife at the bottom.

Your husband or wife should have first place. Your spouse should get your very best. How sad to say on the honeymoon, "Well, here I am, sweetheart. All the leftovers just for you. All these other people have been involved with me, and now I've finally got to you."

Let me ask this. Do you want someone sleeping tonight with your future husband or wife? Then don't you sleep with someone else's spouse.

Teens say to me, "But what happens if I get on the honeymoon and I don't really know what I'm doing? I mean, I don't have any experience, and I don't read so good. What happens then?"

I say you'll have fun practicing! You have a whole lifetime together. It was never meant that two professionals would be coming together. It's supposed to be two novices who love each other.

We are in an instant society. We have instant banking, instant pudding, instant replays, so it's natural to want instant relationships. It's natural to say, "I want to feel good, and I want to feel good now!" We must learn to give up instant gratification for the much deeper satisfaction of developing a healthy me. That's where self-control comes in.

In the past, adults have tried to control teenage sexual urges by laying on teens tremendous feelings of guilt. That's stupid. Guilt does not prevent sexual stimulation. Guilt does not give you positive steps to deal with it, and it usually leads to our developing a poor self-image. Instead we need to stress self-control, which is a positive way of waiting for sex at its very best—in a marriage relationship.

People love to ask, "What if we aren't sexually compatible? Shouldn't we sleep together to discover that?" It sounds like we are talking mechanics here. This isn't like trying to fit a Cadillac engine into a Honda Civic. The wonderful thing is that all the parts fit. If you're worried about this, you can go to a doctor and he can examine both of you. But unless there is some major physical deformity, you don't have to worry.

The quality of sex is not dependent on positions, size, or technique but rather on the quality of the relationship. Good sex comes out of good relationships!

Premarital Sex Will Cause Comparison Problems

You never forget past lovers. The sexual relationship is such an intimate, binding experience that you'll never ever forget them. Now what that does is set up for you the opportunity to compare.

If the sexual relationship after you are married isn't as great as you would like it to be, you begin to think, "He doesn't touch me the way Festus used to touch me," or, "She doesn't kiss me the way Big Bertha used to kiss me." And you become discouraged.

Then there is the worry of whether or not your spouse is thinking about someone else while making love to you—and the concern as to whether you are as good as all the rest.

There isn't supposed to be a comparison. If your relationship isn't as great as you would like it to be, then you work at it to make it better.

YOU GIVE AWAY YOUR VIRGINITY ONE TIME

The world has made a big joke of virginity. It will say, "Are you a virgin? What's the matter with you? You must have some major problem. Come on and lose it!"

Do you know why the world does this? Because it's already lost its virginity. The world can't tell you virginity is important, because then it would feel guilty. So because misery loves company, the world puts pressure on you.

Listen to me. Your virginity is not something to be ashamed of but rather something to be proud of. For you to give your virginity to another is to give your greatest gift. It's to give yourself.

Individuals have said to me, "Intercourse is a sign of maturity. When you finally grow up, then you have sex. That's the sign of a real man or a real woman."

That is the biggest bunch of garbage I've ever heard. However, in a subtle way that is exactly what you hear in your sex education classes. "You've got to be emotionally ready." Well, everybody wants to think he or she is emotionally mature, so we try to prove it by having intercourse.

Give me a break. Two wart hogs can have intercourse. A cow can have intercourse. You don't walk up
to your pet wart hog and say, "What a man! You must
be very mature."

Having intercourse isn't a sign of maturity, but
I'll tell you what is, and that is being able to say NO!
It takes courage, self-discipline, and strength to wait,
and *that* is the sign of a real man or a real woman.

It's OK and good and right to say no. Having high
moral standards doesn't make you weird. And you'll
find that your real friends will stick with you, because
they will allow you to be you.

As you say no to premarital sex, and stick by that
conviction, people will respect you. But let's be honest.
Some individuals may mock and turn away. Realize,
however, that they aren't actually rejecting you. They
just feel bad about themselves.

When you stand for what is right and get your life together, people begin to compare themselves with you—and they don't look so good. They have two choices: get their lives together (that would be hard and take a lot of work), or they can try to tear you down (which is much easier, and misery loves company).

Say no. Stand for what is right. Being a virgin is something to be proud of. You've got everything to gain, and all you lose is fake friends and dates from people who are only after your body.

You May Develop a Taste for Variety

If you have had sexual experience—or if the person you marry has had—what makes you think that now you or your partner will be interested in one sexual partner till death do you part? Research has shown there's a correlation between those who were involved in premarital sex and those who are now involved in adultery.

One of you may have developed a taste for variety. New experiences, different bodies, exciting conquests can in time lure a person away from an otherwise good marriage. In many cases the individual wishes he would not yield to temptation, but the urge is so strong and the past so vivid that he is pulled into sin.

Also remember that a virgin can imagine what it would be like to be involved sexually with a person, but once one has been involved, imagining is no longer necessary. He has been there! So the temptation becomes even stronger for someone who has been sexually active.

Involvement in premarital sex can cause you to see sex as trivial. You'll find yourself saying, "It's no big deal." You have really robbed yourself, because sex is one of the most exciting experiences in life.

YOU LOSE AN OBJECTIVE VIEW OF THE RELATIONSHIP

When you go out with a person, you get to know him or her spiritually, emotionally, and intellectually. You begin to develop open communication.

HOW WELL YOU KNOW EACH OTHER

	1 2 3 4 5 6 7 8 . . .
Spiritual	————→
Emotional	——————→
Intellectual	—————→
Communication	————————→

Then you ask, "Do you love me?"
"Well, I love you."
So you decide to sleep together. Now suddenly you know each other very well physically:

HOW WELL YOU KNOW EACH OTHER

	1 2 3 4 5 6 7 8 . . .
Physical	——————————→

All of a sudden you say, "I feel we are so close. I feel we know each other so well." But this is a false feeling, because there is a gap between where you feel you are and where you are in reality.

HOW WELL YOU KNOW EACH OTHER

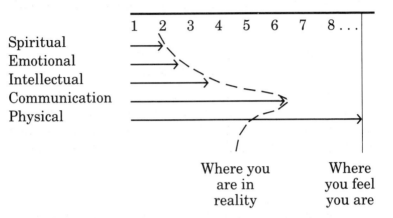

What is an indication that this is happening? Couples come to me and say, "Greg, I feel we should be so close, but we always fight, have stupid arguments. If we aren't having sex, then we are having a hard time getting along." The answer is that you have fooled yourself and settled for a cheap imitation of intimacy.

When you become sexually involved, suddenly you can lose an objective view of the relationship. You may become very subjective, or feeling-oriented. You begin to do things that you never would have dreamed of doing a few months before. You become rebellious. You won't listen to anyone who has anything negative to say about that other person. You lie. You sneak behind other people's backs. You deceive. And what is your excuse? "I'm in love."

Stop to think a moment. Is that what real love causes you to do? The answer is no, and if this is what is happening to you, then you need HELP! Listen to your parents and others around you, because they can see the situation more objectively. Get away from the relationship for a while. Stop having sex. All these things will help you to see the relationship more realistically.

PREMARITAL SEX PREVENTS YOUR DEVELOPING
IN OTHER IMPORTANT AREAS

Premarital sex has a tendency to block the very thing it was meant to promote in a marriage relationship. At first you both think, "This is great. It has really pulled us together." But in many cases after a while things begin to change.

☐ The spiritual area.
Obviously the spiritual area went right down the tubes as soon as you started messing around. Within marriage a good sex life is pleasing to God and helps our spiritual development. But for a dating couple, sex has just the opposite effect. It kills the spiritual dimension of the relationship. You can't tell God you love Him and then continually, willfully, disobey.
☐ The emotional area.
I've already explained the gap between where we feel we are and where we are in reality. Emotionally we are on a roller coaster that goes from extreme highs, where we are so much in love, to ultimate lows, where we are depressed and hate the relationship.
☐ The intellectual area.
Usually we are not much interested in pursuing the intellectual area. Finding out what a person thinks, where he stands, and what he believes in is often overlooked. Because we are attracted to the physical, it is much easier to be physically involved than to get to know what the other person thinks.

Develop the intellectual dimension of your relationship. For example, read the paper together—other than the funnies and sports—and then talk about what you've read. How do you feel about what you've read? Do you agree? Disagree?

It's not as easy as making out, but now you are coming to really know the person.

☐ Communication.

"We just don't talk like we used to. When we do talk it ends up in an argument." Why? Because we have substituted sex for communication.

What happens is that the whole relationship begins to center on sex. We go to a ball game: "Come on, get over, don't go into overtime! Great, let's get out of here." Then we have to go out and eat a little something. "Hurry, shovel the hamburger in! Suck down the fries! Good. Now at the same time drink

your Pepsi. *Phew.* Finally we're done. Now we can go park and have sex."

It is easy for there to be loss of respect. We lose respect for ourselves. We lose respect for the other person. We become unhappy. We want to stop, but we feel trapped on this physical merry-go-round. The relationship begins to fall apart. Eventually we feel used instead of loved, and finally we break up. If we could only start over.

"But, Greg, I never know what to talk about!"

Remember that everyone's favorite subject is himself or herself. Find out what your date is interested in, and ask questions about that.

Or ask each other this: "What are three things that happened to you today, and how did you feel about them?"

Communication may not come easy, but you must be able to communicate openly and honestly to have a healthy relationship.

PREMARITAL SEX KILLS CREATIVITY IN EXPRESSING LOVE

Once we get involved sexually we tend to rely on sex as a way of expressing our love for the other person. But there are many other ways of loving. Some examples:

☐ Use words.

Words are an important way to express love. Tell them how much you care for them. Compliment them. Build their self-worth. Sing them a love song. Phone at a special time.

☐ Spend time together.

Take a walk. Play tennis. Go out to eat. Go shopping. Listen to music. Ski together. Do a service project. Go horseback riding. Play miniature golf.

Go to a concert. You can think of 101 other things you could do. This way you can truly get to know the other person because of the time that is spent together in various settings.

☐ Give gifts.

For no special reason give something the person would enjoy. It's not Christmas, Valentine's Day, your birthday, or Ground Hog Day, but here's a little gift to say I care about you, you're special. You can make a gift. You can give flowers, candy, a key chain, a stuffed animal, a can of tennis balls. Write them poems. Send them fun cards and love letters. When you give a gift you are saying to that person, "I have been thinking about you even when we are not together."

☐ Be helpful.

Help your friend with homework by explaining how to do it. Help with housework, gardening, mowing the lawn, delivering papers. Help with some work, or even do it, so that the person can make a special appointment. This is saying, "I care about you!"

These are just a few ways you can express your caring apart from the physical. There are literally hundreds of things you can do. You are only limited by your imagination and creativity.

CERTAIN DISEASES ARE SEXUALLY TRANSMITTED

I'm not going to go into this in detail, but you are aware that certain diseases are sexually transmitted. The obvious one is AIDS, which is now a heterosexual disease. A young lady, who in the past was sexually active with several different partners, said, "The days of casual sex are over, if you value your life at all!"

Twenty to thirty years ago we had basically two sexually transmitted diseases. Today there are more than twenty-five. Be aware that when you have intercourse with anyone, you are actually having intercourse with everyone your partner has been with for the past seven years. That is the length of time it takes some sexually transmitted diseases to show up.

People are trying to tell you that you can have absolutely safe sex if the man uses a condom. That is a lie. Condom use will cut down risk, but it is not 100 percent safe. The only way to guarantee absolute safety is to abstain.

PREMARITAL SEX WILL WRECK YOUR HONEYMOON

Your honeymoon was meant to be the wonderful and exciting time when you come to know each other sexually. Supposedly you have developed those other areas of your relationship already, so that all that is left is the physical. If you have already been involved sexually, you have removed a lot of the magic of the honeymoon. You will not be doing anything you haven't done before.

This may surprise you, but very few individuals come to me and say, "I wish I would have messed around more when I was in high school and college. I just wish I had had more experience going into this marriage." As a matter of fact, I've never heard that, but I do hear a lot of, "Greg, if only I hadn't been so stupid! Why didn't I wait? I wish I could do it over again, because I would do it so differently."

Premarital sex can cause sexual dysfunctions after you are married. Let's suppose that as a woman you believed strongly that you shouldn't climax with anyone until after you were married. However, you were involved sexually. You just made sure that you stopped before climaxing.

Now you get married, and you're on your honeymoon. You begin to move toward a climax that first night, and then all of a sudden your body turns off. Why? Because you've programmed it to do just that. You become frustrated, he becomes frustrated, and now we have a problem that didn't have to be if we had only waited.

People usually suffer through this type of situation for a while, hoping it will clear up on its own. However, the stress and tensions build, making it even harder to respond. Now you're stuck in this vicious cycle, and if counseling is not started soon, the relationship is at risk of breaking up.

Premarital Sex Doesn't Lead to Emotional Stability

Our culture forces us to grow up much too fast. We are bombarded by sex on TV, on radio, in magazines, in movies. Intellectually we understand the sexual act and the mechanics involved. Socially we are advanced, and we certainly have the possibility of willing partners. Physically we're developed, and our bodies can function sexually. Our parents work, we have access to a car. There are always parties going on, so a place is really no problem. I guess I'm ready, right? WRONG!

We forget one crucial area, and that is our emotional side. Now most teenagers like to think of themselves as mature. When I ask a teen, "Are you mature emotionally?" I have very few who say, "Nope, I'm pretty squirrelly."

Now I know this will tick off some of you, but I feel I need to speak the truth in love and tell you that as a teenager you're just not ready for sex emotionally.

Emotional maturity only comes with time and growing up. You aren't as mature at seventeen as you will be at twenty-five or as you will be at forty-five. With emotional maturity come better judgment and understanding.

Your teen years are an emotional roller-coaster ride. Just look at the number of your friends who are unhappy, depressed, suicidal, moody. Premarital sex doesn't lead to emotional stability. Often it does just the opposite. It causes emotional chaos. Even if you love each other very much, have known each other a long time, and have sat down and talked about sex and decided you both want it, you still aren't ready emotionally.

Ask a twenty-five-year-old if there is any difference in his emotional maturity now compared to when he was a teenager. You'll find there are some big changes. If there haven't been changes, then that person is in trouble because he isn't growing.

Emotional maturity will happen as you grow older, so wait, please. Don't give away something now that later on you're going to regret having given away.

I can hear it already: "But we're different. We are very emotionally mature, and we truly love each other. This isn't infatuation."

Almost every couple I meet feels this way. But try for a moment to be objective. (They say love is blind, and there is truth to that. We become so subjectively involved we have difficulty seeing the relationship objectively.)

Look around you, and tell me how many teen relationships are lasting for years. Few of us would think —or want to admit—that our relationship is purely physical. I have heard it said that the average American falls in love seven times.

Now some of you will fall in love only two or three times. Others of you are going to seek to establish a new *Guiness Book of World Records.* Are you going to sleep with every one of those individuals? How can you be sure that this is the one? You wait until marriage!

Now I know that even in marriage there is no guarantee that there won't be divorce or adultery, but that is because we don't really understand what love and marriage ought to be.

Love is not just a feeling; it is a commitment. It is something you do whether you feel like it or not. The same should be true of marriage—it is a commitment till death do you part, not till feelings begin to fade.

So we ought to hold off on sex until we commit ourselves to someone for the rest of our lives. That happens in marriage, not in a dating relationship. Feelings change. A commitment stays true.

Let me tell you a little secret. I don't always feel that I love my wife, Bonnie. And Bonnie doesn't always feel that she loves me, because we get mad at each other. But regardless of those occasional feelings, we are committed to one another for better or worse, in sickness and health, for richer, for poorer, till death do us part! That is love.

Trust Is Broken

Trust becomes broken with the loss of self-control. If your partner can't be trusted to do what's right before marriage, can he or she be trusted to do what's right after marriage?

Remember how convincingly he (or she) lied to his parents? How do we know that we aren't being lied to now? All of a sudden there is suspicion, which can quickly lead to possessiveness and jealousy.

PREMARITAL SEX CAN LEAD TO PREGNANCY

I won't spend much time here on the subject of pregnancy. A whole chapter on the topic is coming up. But don't let anyone tell you that with birth control you can't get pregnant—that is a lie. The only sure way of not getting pregnant is using self-control.

So when "friends" say to you, "Hey, how come you're not sleeping around? What's the matter? You weird? Scared? Gay? Come on, I do it because everybody else is doing it. Can you give me one good reason why you aren't?" tell them, "No, I don't have one good reason. I have twelve!"

Major changes can occur in this country in the area of sexuality. I believe those changes can begin with teenagers, and I would like to see them start with you.

But you've got to decide. You need to start making decisions with your head and not with your hormones. Your parents, teachers, pastors, and friends can't make those decisions for you.

Yes, I believe that you, controlled by the Holy Spirit, can do whatever is right.

5

What Other Teens Say
(A Word from Your Peers)

"I met this guy at a roller skating rink. . . ."

Premarital sex will cause you far more emotional pain than it will ever give you physical pleasure. And the Word of God is specific about some of the problems that go along with it. Let's take a look at four Scripture passages. But instead of my trying to stress the importance of what the Bible says, we'll hear from some of your peers who have written about their experiences.

1 PETER 2:11

"Dear friends, I urge you, as aliens and strangers in the world, to abstain from sinful desires, which war against the soul."

Premarital sex will rob you of peace. Or, another way to put it is that in the long run you will be miserable.

You who have been involved, or are now involved, know that premarital sex takes away your peace. There is so much guilt, confusion, and anxiety going on inside of you. You can't very well say you love Jesus Christ and then disgrace Him at the same time. You become two-faced, acting one way around your

73

Christian friends and parents and another way around your partner.

Look at Psalm 51:3. It says, "My sin is always before me." That's true, isn't it? Even though we rationalize and try to come up with good excuses, it still is there before us. We know it's wrong, and it slowly eats away at us from the inside out.

John 10:10 tells us that Christ came so that we could experience life in its fullness. We are missing out on that exciting, abundant life because we are compromising and in turn being robbed.

Now listen to what seven of your peers have to say.

☐ "I loved him so much that it just felt right to have sex together. But after we broke up, I have become so guilty. He doesn't even know this, but I was pregnant when he broke it off. I was so depressed. I tried to kill myself. The next day I had a miscarriage. Oh, Greg, I killed my baby. For so long I have cried, and I feel this pain deep down in my heart. I expect I always will."

☐ "At camp I met this guy, and we spent the whole week together. Toward the end of the week we got a chance to be alone, and we started out with just kissing. Then his hands began to wander. We never went all the way, but we got involved in heavy petting. He said he loved me, but the next day we had to leave, and he didn't even say good-bye. After I got home I called him, and he was very cold and short with me. It seemed so beautiful at the time, but now I feel awful."

☐ "What's wrong with me? People told me not to have sex, but I did anyway. Now I find that I just let guys use me and treat me really bad. No one understands why I do that, and I'm not too sure if I can really understand it either. It seems to me that guys look at me like I'm an object. Whenever I'm out with my friends or the youth group, there is always at least one guy who will try to pick me up."

☐ "Awhile back I had an affair with a girl. Not because I loved her or because she loved me, but because it was something to do, and it felt good. Afterwards I was so guilty, I was miserable on the inside, and it affected my relationships with others. I was angry and rude toward others. I began to give in to lust, which only depressed me more.

"I finally talked with someone, and I'm on my way back. I want to be a missionary and really serve God. This was a terrible mistake that I'll never make again."

☐ "I met this guy at a roller skating rink. We were too young to date, but I would see him once a week at the rink. After a month he invited me to his house. . . . His parents were gone, and he wanted to have sex with me. I really wanted to say no, but I was afraid of losing him, so I said yes. A week later we started to fight, and he broke up.

"I feel so crushed! The love turned to lust, and the lust to nothing. I feel so empty inside. I want a guy that will love me the person, not the body. I want someone I can love and someone to respect me. Am I asking too much?"

☐ "Please tell people to wait to have sex, because the pleasure is not worth the pain. We were going to be different. We loved each other. We were mature. We even used birth control. She got pregnant, and now we're married, and I'm only seventeen.

"I'm working, trying to get my GED, be a husband, and be a father. How can I be a father? I still want to be a kid. I don't even think I love her, and now it's for the rest of my life. I sometimes wonder what God could have done with my life."

☐ " 'I love you!' That's what he told me. We spent all our time together, but it wasn't great. Twice we thought I was pregnant. I went to bed with him for two months—so very young. Then he left, and now I feel like he never really cared. I am still so hurt. Even after four months I still cry because it's so painful. I've been used, and he lied to me to get something he wanted.

"In two days it will be our six-month anniversary. Does he even remember? I cry and wish I were still a virgin. I wish I had never done it. I've lost something I will never get back again. Only after it's too late do I know the value of virginity."

ISAIAH 59:2

"Your iniquities have separated you from your God; your sins have hidden his face from you, so that he will not hear."

Premarital sex will damage your relationship with God. After coming home from a date where you have sought each other's body, you're not going to want to seek after God. Your relationship with Him will begin to slide, because you're more interested in pleasing man than in pleasing God.

Listen to these five teenagers:

☐ "Everyone said what a great Christian I was and how God was going to use me. Then I met this girl, and soon my interest in God became less and less, and she became more and more important. We started having intercourse, and now she is pregnant. Do I marry her? If I could only start over again. I want to be used by God. That's when I was the happiest."

☐ "Although I know God has forgiven me, I can't seem to shake the guilt. I regret this ever happened. All I want to do is get rid of this guilt and start over with the Lord. Why can't I do this? It seems as if my relationship with the Lord is totally shattered."

☐ "Pretty soon he was asking me to do stuff with him that I knew God said no to. So I kept saying no until I finally felt I was ready. It didn't make our relationship better. In fact, it made it worse, and about two weeks later we broke up. I feel like God and I are strangers."

☐ "I was thinking about what you said about being able to go back in time and being able to do things different and would we like to. I have made so

many mistakes. Over and over I ask God to forgive me, and you say He forgives and forgets. But I can't forget.

"Greg, I feel terrible about myself—things I've done and how I am. I'm so far away from God, and I'm going to have to live with my past until I die and maybe even after that. I am so depressed because I am about as low as they come. I've lost track of the number of guys I've made love to. I'm spoiled rotten. I'm obnoxious, and worst of all I killed my baby.

"I thought of only myself when I had the abortion. Only myself. How can God forgive me? How can I forgive myself? I've thought of jumping off the nearest bridge. I'm so confused. Please help me if you can."

☐ "I can't even believe that I'm writing to you about this, because I never thought it would happen to me. My boyfriend and I have been dating for two years now. At first everything was great, and he really loved the Lord. We had made plans to get married, and I loved him so much that I couldn't imagine being without him.

"But after a year, things started to change. We started doing a little petting, but I kept stopping it, and he would get frustrated and angry. He decided to break off the relationship. Our physical relationship had interfered with our relationship with God. We were both confused and depressed, and we felt even farther away from God.

"We decided to get back together again, but our relationship is so different now. We never talk about God anymore. I needed him so much that I let him touch me wherever he wanted. When we were together I didn't care what we did. I loved him and wanted to show him how much I loved him, so one evening we made love. After that we have been making love a lot.

"I have completely drawn away from Jesus, and I haven't been to church in a long time. I guess I have a new god—sex! But Greg, I know he is going to break up with me soon. I can't handle it, and I'm scared I'll do something stupid. I have no one to talk to because I gave up all my friends for him. "You're the only one I have. Please help me, Greg. I never would have dreamed that I would ever be in this mess. How could I have done this? Oh, God, I'm going crazy."

EPHESIANS 4:19

"Having lost all sensitivity, they have given themselves over to sensuality so as to indulge in every kind of impurity, with a continual lust for more." You will lose sensitivity to the Holy Spirit. How do I know that? Because you'll begin to rationalize that what you are doing really is OK—you are "different from everybody else." By continuing in your sin you will sear your conscience and lose sensitivity to spiritual matters.

Wrong will begin to seem right. You'll lie to your parents, get involved in other sin, reject your friends, become rebellious, and all this will seem right to you.

Premarital sex never really satisfies, even though it feels good for the moment. The desire becomes insatiable. The more you get, the more you want. You always want to go farther and farther. The pain becomes deeper and deeper.

☐ "It's hard to believe I'm only seventeen. My friends and I started asking a lot about sex, and it sounded pretty fun to me. Last year I started going out with

this non-Christian guy even though I knew it was wrong.

"I started thinking about having intercourse with him right away. I'm a Christian, but the more physical we got the farther away God seemed. We finally had intercourse and continued to have it for two months.

"After we broke up I started dating other guys, but I can't control myself physically. Now I sleep with everyone I go out with. Every time I come home I make these promises to stop, but I never do. My reputation is so bad, and guys just date me now because they want sex. How can I stop? I'm so scared!"

☐ "I'm enjoying myself. Sure there are problems, but then again that's nothing new. Drinking and sex is fun. Actually the biggest reason I go to dances is to find someone I can have sex with, and that's not too hard.

"I haven't given much thought to God, and you're right, I'm still suicidal at times. But sometimes I'm just . . . life, I don't care anymore. Thank God I haven't had intercourse yet! Once I was very near to it though, and I hardly even knew the guy I was rolling on the ground with.

"I've been involved with five different guys in the past five weekends. Yes, I'm disgusting, I know. I know. A big piece of meat that people can use."

☐ "A friend of mine set me up with an old boyfriend of hers. We hit it right off in the beginning. At first I stuck by my standards—no sex before marriage. Well, one day I dropped them. I didn't care. It wasn't long before I regretted that decision. All we did was have intercourse. That's all he wanted to do.

"I tried to deceive myself and convince myself it was OK. I lied to other people and myself. I started to believe that what I was doing wasn't wrong, because we were going to get married. We never set a date, but it was part of our future plans. Well, he just decided he wanted to break up and told me he had cheated on me. What did I do?"

☐ "I'm supposed to be this really good Christian girl. I go to a Christian high school where I'm a cheerleader and a member of the Honor Society. I'm even an officer in my youth group, but it's all a joke. I started going out with this Christian guy, and we both fell deeply in love.

"My parents weren't thrilled, because he was five years older than me. My parents wanted us to just be friends, but pretty soon my whole life began to center around him.

"I convinced myself that my parents didn't really understand me or the situation, so it was OK to lie to them. We talked about how much we loved each other and sex. We both agreed that we wanted to wait till marriage to have intercourse, but our relationship was different. We were so close and such good friends that it was like we were married, and we got along better than our parents.

"So one night I lied about staying at a friend's house and went to his house. His parents were gone. We decided that sex was OK because we would get married someday. We really loved each other, and both of us were virgins. It was wonderful, and I didn't feel bad or guilty. I was ecstatic, and I had never been happier in my whole life. Now we were married in God's eyes.

"We started making love a lot, but each time it became less and less perfect. It began to feel cold, and each time was faster than the other. I told him that I was feeling used, and this upset him a lot. We began to fight, and he decided we needed to be apart for a while.

"Now he's dating another girl, and it turns out that he had had sex with three girls before me."

□ "We were such good friends that it didn't matter that he wasn't a Christian. My mother was against the relationship, and that made me so mad. He told me everything, and we trusted each other completely.

"After a month, one night he said that he didn't want to have sex but he just wanted to feel close to me, so he wanted to lie on his bed with me with our clothes off. I don't know what I was thinking or if I was thinking, but we did that and nothing happened.

"A week later we went back to his room, and this time we had sex. It was like I was so blind that I couldn't listen to my parents or my friends. He broke up with me and told the basketball team everything we had done."

GALATIANS 5:19

"The acts of the sinful nature are obvious: sexual immorality, impurity and debauchery."
One sin tends to lead to another.

☐ "My boyfriend and I were just sexually attracted to each other. My parents told me to stay away from him, but I snuck around and lied to them so I could see him. He was older and could get drugs. We spent most of our time in his bedroom. Then to make things worse, I got pregnant. He said he would pay for an abortion, and it seemed like the best way out at the time. He soon broke up with me. I guess we never really loved each other anyway. I've never told my parents. They would have hit the ceiling."

☐ "I have sex with men but only after I am drunk, because it's easier that way. I'm nineteen years old, and I want a good relationship. But I don't know how to start or what to do. Please help me."

☐ "I'm married now, but before I was engaged my husband and I started having intercourse. He loved me, but I wasn't sure I loved him. We were having sex every night, and this really hurt and confused our relationship. But that was the only way we could show our love for each other, because we couldn't communicate.

"But instead of getting closer we were fighting all the time. There was also the fear of getting pregnant. It was terrible, and we finally decided to either stop or break up. We stopped, and two months later we got married.

"Our wedding night wasn't anything that I had ever dreamed of. It wasn't like it was supposed to be, because we had already wrecked it. If there is anyone else in this situation, I would say wait. If I had to do it over again I would have waited to have sex until after marriage.

"Some girls think if you don't give, then he'll dump you. But I think that if he really loves you, he'll understand. Well, Greg, I hope this will help someone."

☐ "I remember you saying that there is a war going on inside your life between your old and new natures. And the nature that wins out is the one you feed the most. Well, I've been feeding my old nature, and I'm really in trouble.

" When I was fifteen my parents brought this girl into our house who was an unwed mother. She was nineteen. After the baby was born she gave it up for adoption but continued to live with us, because her parents wouldn't let her back in. We became good friends, and one afternoon when my parents were gone she came into my room, and we had intercourse.

"This was my first time, and we made love for one year, and I thought I loved her and wanted to get married. My parents had no idea what was going on. After a year she moved in with two other guys and left me.

"I was really mad. I forgot about God and really got into pornography. At seventeen I met this fifteen-year-old girl, and we made love for six months. I never really loved her, but she wanted to marry me.

Now I'm involved with another girl, and all I really care about is her body.

"I know this is wrong, but I feel like I'm out of control and my old nature is leading me. I know I need Jesus. I want to stop. Please help me, because I'm so scared that I've permanently messed up my life."

☐ "I've really lived a wild life when my parents and people from church and school aren't around. I hated myself and had attempted suicide several times. I had even considered prostitution.

"I see now that I have to let go of the past and let Christ change my life. Thanks for talking with me. I came to the conference seriously considering ending my life, but now I have a reason to live."

These teens would tell you that the pleasure is not worth the price. Do you want to go through all this? You don't have to learn the hard way. Listen to your peers, and don't make the same mistakes.

Read that last letter again. Maybe you think it's too late for you. But that's not true. There is hope and a fresh start waiting for you, if you'll give your life to Jesus Christ. He's the one who gives us a reason to live.

6

What God Can Do
(Should I Tell My Parents?)

*Her mother saw the business envelope
and thought it was junk mail. . . .* □

I love to watch the wonderful ways in which God
works.

God desires to work in and through our families.
On the whole, we do not appreciate our parents
enough. We don't think that they will understand
what we are going through.

But parents have tremendous wisdom, and in the
majority of cases they love us very much. That means
we ought to be going to our parents more often with
our needs and problems.

Here is a letter I received from a teenager. She
had not told her parents what was happening in her
life. She wanted to work through it herself, but God
had a better idea!

LETTER A

Dear Greg Speck:
If you cannot help me, I think I will go utter-
ly out of my mind. My precious walk with Jesus is
constantly being axed down by the number one
weakness in my life, and if I don't gain victory

over it soon, I really believe my insides will be so screwed up that I may even turn my back totally on Jesus out of mere frustration and confusion!

My impossible weakness is sex. By sex I mean from heavy kissing all the way up to that precious gift God gave us of making love.

Oh, Greg, it hurts so bad! I want to quit so much. I want to live for my Lord so bad! But my stupid desires keep tripping me up. And I am sick of it. Yet I cannot give them up. I've prayed, oh, so earnestly. Yet I keep selfishly taking back what I give. . . . I really wanted to talk to you so badly, but I was afraid. . . .

The talks you gave on sex were so meaningful to me. And one thing that has remained in my mind and heart was when you said, "Once you've petted, once you've gone so far, it's so hard to go back again."

Well, I think I disagreed with that then, since my boyfriend and I had gone a few steps too many. I was so all out to prove you wrong (subconsciously). Yet, looking back, everywhere I turned, everything we tried, failed.

I am 18, my boyfriend is 20. We've been dating on and off for about 3 years and up until a few months ago we had done everything (physically) except go all the way. Never once did he pressure me. Never once did he even nudge me, but over all those months, my once strong-willed ability to say no weakened and weakened.

Now, we've done it 3 times. Special? I don't know. I don't see us getting married, because he is not a spiritual leader and Christ has never really been #1 for him. But Greg, I still hang on to him. Why? I love being with him. I love him as a person, and I care so much for him and I pray and hope that someday he can be a spiritual leader and be on fire for Christ! But I am not in love with him.

Oh, we've broken up and had cooling off periods, but I always let us come together again. In fact, we're in a cooling off situation now. But it isn't working. I know what I have to do. But I can't do it.

Greg, I really don't know what I'm asking from you. You must have so many burdens and problems to deal with that I'm just another one of those in the sex category. That's understandable, but to me this is the most devastating thing that has ever happened to me in my life. I'm me, and I thank God for making me the way He did. But look what I've done and keep on doing.

I am so disappointed in myself. I never ever thought I would make love before I was married. I promised myself. I was secure in that. And I believe I am a strong-willed person.

But now I may have caused bad memories for my boyfriend and hurt feelings in his future wife. And the same goes for me. When I'd hear of other girls doing it, it was so distant for my understanding. Now *I'm* dealing with it. And I hate it.

I am such a dirtbag, sleazy, slimey, dirty-minded sinner.

And Greg, I am a leader in my youth group and looked up to by kids as well as by adults!

If they only knew me! I am on fire for Jesus except when my desires come around. They always take over.

I know I am forgiven, but how can I really stop? How can I get away from my boyfriend and *hold to it?* Please don't say trust in Jesus, 'cuz I have. It just seems to dwindle.

I am so weak here!

A struggling sister,

Well, I wrote back sharing some steps she could begin to take to reestablish purity. (Check out chapter 13 for what I said.)

Now I sent my reply to her home address, but in the meantime she had left for college. Her mother saw the business envelope and thought it was junk mail. She was about to throw it out but decided that she had better open it, just in case it was something important. She started to read and—well, listen to the mother. She can do a much better job of explaining than I can.

Here is the letter that the mom wrote to her daughter:

LETTER B

Dear _____

[Two letters came in the mail for you today.]
And I didn't really pay too much attention to
them, figuring they were just ads or more re-
quests for money, etc. At first I was just going to
throw them both away, but decided I'd better
check them out first just to be sure they weren't
important, or if maybe I should keep them for you
until you came home again.

I honestly wish now that I hadn't opened the
one, but I couldn't *un-open* it, especially since I
just ripped it open, and once I had read it far
enough to figure out if it was important, there
was no use trying to pretend I didn't understand
what it was all about.

Please believe me, I never intended to "snoop"
or read something that personal. Even if I had
stopped reading after the first page, it was too
late. And with the envelope ripped so badly, there
was just no way to pretend I didn't understand
what Greg Speck was writing about.

I did read all the letter. My heart was beating
so fast. I kept hoping that I had misunderstood
and that if I kept reading I'd find out that the
guilt you wrote him about was for sinful thoughts
or desires, and when I finished reading it, I guess
I just felt numb. I think I still do.

There is so much I wish I could say to you,
and of course I can understand why you couldn't
come to me. But I feel so bad knowing that you
carried this guilt around and finally had to write
to someone you respected and could trust with
your secret.

I don't know when this happened, and it isn't
important for me to know. . . . I guess you've been
carrying this guilt for quite a while. . . .

The advice that he gives you seems like very good advice, and I hope, since you asked for advice, that you will really consider and pray about his advice. It's definitely not *easy* advice, and the toughest part about it is that he's asking you to honestly face what happened and why. That means you may have to relive the guilt just at a time when you had maybe hoped to put those feelings behind you.

I guess I am also going to have to say some things you may not want to hear either.

When you were home last weekend, I guess I was disappointed to come home and find you lying on the couch with [him]. This is something I have mentioned to you before (many times), and I have always felt that this is not a good habit to get into with any boy. . . . I understand that it sounds silly to call it dangerous, but . . . one step just naturally leads to another, and guys just can't handle that much intimacy very long. Neither can girls.

After reading the letter from Greg S., I guess I'm really trying to understand why you even allowed yourself to get on the couch with him this past weekend. . . . I know that God promises that He will "not allow anyone to be tempted beyond what he is able to bear, but will with the temptation provide an escape," but honey, God expects you to use your sense and not give Satan a chance to tempt you. . . .

Decide once and for all that whether you are with [him] or some other guy, you simply will not do anything that you would be ashamed [of]. . . .

Finally, honey, I want you to know that I love you very much, and my feelings of respect for you have not changed. You made a mistake, and I know you are really disappointed with yourself and probably even feel your relationship with God can never be quite the same again.

But now is when you have to really place all your . . . trust in the promises in the Bible, [which] you know are true. "If [when] you confess your sin, He is faithful and just to forgive you your sin and cleanse you from all unrighteousness." God promises that He will forgive and forget, and you need to say Thank You Lord and get up and start all over brand new.

I'd like to tell you that if God forgets it, then you need to forget it too—but that's not going to happen. You do need to forget it as far as not dwelling on it [is concerned] and doing everything in your power to push it out of your mind whenever it comes back. Satan would love it if you kept dwelling on your guilt and trying to analyze how and why it happened. If he can keep you feeling guilty it will also keep you from reestablishing your relationship with God.

And eventually a person who refuses to forgive himself will try to find ways to excuse . . . or justify [himself]. It may take years before you find you can get through even one single day without remembering your sin, but it will happen. Do I sound like a person who has gone through a little guilt in my life? I am!

One more thing, and then I promise I will be done. I think I can understand now why going to [school] and getting away was so important and why you were so convinced that this was also God's will for you. When the guilt comes back, think about how faithful God was to provide that escape for you. He really did work a miracle for you.

Be sure that you don't fool yourself into thinking that just seeing [your friend] "less often" will solve everything.

God has given you the chance to really put Step 3 in Greg's letter into practice. . . . You've only been gone for 3 weeks, and yet you have been home once—with [him]—and this weekend [he] will be there. If God has provided a way of escape . . . you can't keep opening the door of temptation. You seem to be still trying to handle this in your own wisdom.

Don't you see that Greg is right—you need to make a complete break for at least 6 months to give God a chance to help both [of you]. In your heart . . . you know that [he] is spiritually weak, and I'm sure you've convinced yourself that maybe you're not so spiritually strong yourself.

And maybe you aren't as strong as you thought you were. But two spiritually weak people will never make one spiritually strong person. *You* can't give [him] the strength he needs. Only God can do that. You can't do that for [him] any more than I can do it for you. All I can do is remind you of what you already know.

If Satan hasn't already tried, he will try to convince you that you have spoiled any chance of waiting for God's best. Or he will try to convince you that [this boy] is God's best.

You know Satan is a liar, and God still wants His very best for you. Maybe it will be [him], or maybe it will be a minister, but you have to let go of [him] and open the doors again for God to work in your life. I don't care what's happened in the past with [him]. You don't owe [him] anything, but you owe God everything.

Please keep in contact with Greg Speck. Just having someone to write to about your struggles and doubts is going to help a lot. Greg could be the other escape God is offering. When you are really serious about only accepting God's best, God will keep offering help and He'll send people into your life to keep encouraging you.

I love you, honey,

Mom

Shortly after "Mom" wrote that letter, I received another note from the college girl. Here is a young lady excited! Why? Because she is seeing God work in her life through her family.

As you read this letter, I pray that God will soften your heart toward your own parents.

LETTER C

Dear Greg,

I want to thank you so much for writing back when you did. The timing was all in the Lord's will, and you could not even begin to realize how your one letter has been used this weekend.

I wish so much I could talk to you face to face and just give you the biggest hug, and cry with you in joy!

Let me try to give you the whole picture because this truly is a miracle!

I'm going to college [and when your letter came] my mom opened it thinking it was more mail from other ministries, wondering whether she should send it to me or not. She read your whole letter, Greg, and my secret I'd ached with for so long crept into her, and she found out about it all.

In the meantime, [my boyfriend] was going to come up for the weekend so we could spend some time together (obviously we hadn't totally given each other up to the Lord yet). My mom gave him an envelope to give to me. In it was a letter to me and one to him. . . .

Greg, I cannot believe this happened. After reading my mom's letter, I was so relieved, so relieved, that she finally knew. The horror and pain was finally beginning to lift. My mom and I are very close, and I tell her everything but could not come to her with this problem.

I hope I'm not hogging your time by writing so much, but this is so beautiful the way it happened! I cannot thank you enough, Greg. [My boyfriend] and I thought a lot this weekend. We avoided the topic at first but then really had a good talk. We are going to take your advice, Greg. We are going to cut off our relationship. No letters, no phone calls, no seeing each other when I come home—for 6 months at least.

Greg, this is what I've been waiting for! I've heard the Lord telling me to break up and serve Him fully for so long! But I didn't obey. I didn't obey! And now, through all this hurt and pain, the terrible pain I've caused my mom, the awful hurt of really letting go of [him] and knowing I won't see him for so long, all of this hurts so bad, but God finally got through. I finally said, "Okay, Lord, it's yours. Take it."

He had to pound me over the head. But I finally yielded, Greg! And it is wonderful. All my burdens are off of me. My horrible sin is gone! It doesn't haunt me anymore!

Greg, this is the most traumatic thing that's ever happened to me in my life. I've never cried so much as I have this weekend. But I've never felt so happy and relieved either. This is really a big stepping-stone in my relationship to God—and I am so excited. I know it's going to be so hard, but I'm leaning on Him.

I prayed that He would hold me up by both of my armpits, 'cuz I don't think I can do it any other way. I know I can't. I need all of my Lord's strength. . . .

Oh, and you asked about using parts of my letter for your book. Please use whatever you want. My heart goes out to so many girls, and I want them to make the right decision and to remain pure and to not make the mistake I did! If anything could be helpful, I want you to use it. . . .

I have the best mom in the whole world, and I love her so much.

I'm rejoicing in Him too! In Christ's wonderful love,

God so desires to work in your life as well. Read the last part of her letter again. She doesn't want you to go through what she has gone through, and neither do I.

So have a love affair with Jesus Christ. The pleasure you will get from being with, being used by, and being loved by the King of kings and Lord of lords will far surpass any love affair with another person.

Even if you're involved sexually now, it's not too late. Remember secondary virginity, which says, "Yes,

I've done it, but from now on I'm seeking to glorify Christ with my body."

It's never too late, but why go through another day of pain when you could be free?

FALL IN LOVE WITH JESUS! He is Someone you can be with every moment of every day. He will listen to you. He loves you. And He won't dump you!

7

It Can't Be Happening to Me
(Pregnancy—And What to Do Now)

What am I going to do? □

"The test was positive. This can't be happening to me. Other people get pregnant, but I never thought I would. What am I going to do? What will Bill think? Will he still love me? How am I ever going to tell my parents? If I could only turn back the clock and have a chance to do it all again! I don't want to have a kid—I just want to *be* a kid."

What should she do?
What would you do?
What have you done?

Before I relate some steps this girl can take to get help, let me first tell her and you something you shouldn't do. *Whatever you do, don't get an abortion.*

Immediately the girl thinks, "How can I get out of this as fast as possible with the least amount of embarrassment?" The answer is obviously abortion, and in many cases there is a sense of relief *immediately following*. But women are now coming forward, five to ten years later, having tremendous emotional pain from that decision to have an abortion.

It's hard for me to fathom that we murder our children. And why? Mostly for convenience' sake. We don't want to be bothered by the emotional trauma or the physical discomfort or public humiliation.

101

Look at some children around you today. That is what we are destroying—not a thing, not even a mass of tissue of potential life. This is a life with a soul wanting so badly to live.

Did you know that at about . . .

18 days - the mouth begins to open
24 days - arms and legs are beginning to take shape
42 days - fingers are forming on the hand
67 days - hair is now growing
75 days - the baby is seeing

A miracle is growing inside of you, and you want to kill it? Do you know what I wish? I wish we had a little window to the womb. If you could only see that baby inside of you, which is a part of you, you would never take its life.

The abortion clinic makes it sound so easy. No hassles. Well, it is easy for the doctor, and he is making good money. Some doctors specialize in abortion now. They took an oath to save lives, but they're getting rich murdering babies. Abortion clinics are exploiting women, and you need to know some of the facts.

First understand that you are having surgery, and anytime that happens you run the risk of developing problems. What are some of the physical problems that women are experiencing as a result of abortion?

☐ Damage to the cervix
☐ Increased possibility of miscarrying later on
☐ Premature births
☐ Tubal pregnancies
☐ Painful perforation of the uterus
☐ Inability to have children
☐ Infections

In addition, at least 50 percent of all individuals who go into an abortion clinic never come out alive. They say it's a safe procedure for you, but it's deadly for your baby.

Would you like to know what your child goes through if it is aborted? Well, here are the four main techniques, but I warn you that this isn't pretty and reading about them could cause some emotional trauma, especially if you've already had an abortion:

☐ Dilatation and Curettage.

In the dilatation and curettage method, you first will have several shots at the mouth of the womb to deaden the area so that the pain and discomfort are relieved for you—but not for the baby. They will have to dilate your cervix with a variety of instruments.

Then they will take the curette, a long instrument shaped like a spoon, and push it into the uterus. Your baby is then mashed and smashed into pieces and scraped from the wall of the uterus.

Now are you ready for this? The assisting nurse must put the parts together again to make sure they got everything so that you won't get infected. At this point the baby doesn't have to worry about infection. As you can imagine, there is usually a lot of bleeding.

☐ Vacuum Aspiration.

In vacuum aspiration, once again they need to get your cervix dilated. But this time they insert a tube into your uterus. This is better, you think. But it isn't.

This instrument is like a vacuum cleaner in that it sucks your baby out of the uterus—but not in one piece. The suction is so strong that your child is ripped to pieces and deposited in a jar.

It's pretty difficult for the nurse to get all the pieces back together again, because the pieces are torn and we don't have clean cuts. But don't worry. The vacuum usually does a complete job, for we sure wouldn't want you to get any of those infections.

☐ Saline Injection.

I believe saline injection is the worst. This procedure is usually done after four months. Why? Because they need enough fluid in the sac around the baby. They then take a long needle and thrust it through your abdomen into the sac. They will suck out some of the fluid and then inject a salt solution. Your baby begins to swallow this.

Now your child starts to jerk and kick. It is suffering severely, because it is literally being burned alive by the solution inside your womb. If there ever ought to be a safe protected place, it should be your womb. I wish both parents had to watch this procedure.

It will take your child more than an hour to die. I want you to know that in that hour you will feel it fighting and kicking to live, while it suffers horribly.

Usually within twenty-four hours, you will go into labor and deliver this tortured baby, dead. Its skin has been burned away.

But there is another problem. After all that suffering the baby still may be born alive. Imagine wanting to live that much. Your doctor or nurse will sometimes take this poor burned baby and place it in a corner to die. This will be somewhere out of sight, so that you don't have to watch.

Many times they will place a towel over its face so that it suffocates. I think in other situations we would call this murder.

If the doctor would want to, he could save the baby, and it would be put up for adoption. This has happened, but I'm sorry to say it's the exception rather than the rule.

☐ Dilatation and Evacuation.

The dilatation and evacuation procedure is usually performed later in a pregnancy. Plain and simple, they will take what resembles a pair of pliers and cut up the baby piece by piece. The tough part is the head, which is usually the largest part and needs to be crushed to get it out. I remind you that although the discomfort may be minimal for you, it isn't for your baby.

Now let me be honest and tell you that the Surgeon General has said that abortion is a safe procedure, both physically and psychologically. But it seems to me we are seeing more and more women who are struggling emotionally with a past abortion five to seven years down the road.

Here is a poem that was given to my friends Scott and Julie Peterson by a young woman who had an abortion:

> The tables they turned so quickly,
> I was left with no time for thought.
> I'm not sure why I did it,
> For regret is all it brought.
>
> I gave in for their reasons
> Because I had none for myself.
> I heard the life inside me
> Would be gone with nothing left.

> Me and the baby entered together,
> Left alone once we were inside.
> I asked for this last time together
> Before the baby of mine would die.
>
> I wondered if the baby could hear me
> And knew this choice wasn't really mine.
> Then just as I whispered, "I'm sorry,"
> I heard a knock and knew it was time.
>
> The pain I felt had made me scream—
> It was more than I could take—
> But nothing could prepare me
> For the emptiness that took its place.

If I have hurt your feelings, I'm sorry, but that hurt is nothing compared to the hurt caused a child who is aborted.

We are outraged at the clubbing to death of baby seals, and we are crying out to save the whales. Now I agree with these two causes, but let's start with saving the babies.

We need teenagers like you who will be willing to speak out against abortion. Let's face it, we wouldn't dream of treating our dog or cat the way some of us have treated our own flesh and blood.

God speaks of the child growing in the womb as some*one,* not just some*thing.* Please get a Bible and read these verses. Then write down what the Bible says about that unborn child.

> Psalm 139:13-16
> Jeremiah 1:5
> Luke 1:41-44
> Isa. 49:1
> Prov. 24:11-12

Even with all this spelled out, we still try to rationalize. Here are some of the excuses that I hear:

☐ *"What right have you to tell me this? It's my body!"* No, it isn't. Look at 1 Corinthians 6:19-20, "Do you not know that your body is a temple of the Holy Spirit, who is in you, whom you have received from God? You are not your own; you were bought at a price. Therefore honor God with your body."

☐ *"What if my parents or pastor tell me to get an abortion?"* We are to obey our parents unless to do so contradicts the Word of God. You cannot obey your parents by murdering your child. But at the same time, don't be rude. Try to explain as kindly as possible what God is leading you to do. Remember that your parents are in crisis now too. They have what is called parental ego, and they are concerned about how their friends are reacting. This may be embarrassing to them also. As for the pastor, I'm saddened, but he is totally off the wall and wrong in his advice if he recommends abortion.

☐ *"It's better to have an abortion than to have an unloved and unwanted child."* Well, maybe unwanted and unloved by you. But you will find hundreds and hundreds of couples wanting to adopt your child and love it. Get some counseling, love, and support. Allow others to serve you during the time of pregnancy. An alternative can always be to give up the baby for adoption.

☐ *"Even if abortions were illegal, women would get them anyway, and then their lives would be in danger. So it's better to have abortions in a safe, sterile environment."* Let me give you another scenario. A mother wants to kill her three-year-old son, but to do that she has to go into a bad neighborhood where there is a chance that she will get hurt. So what's the solution? Pass a law so that she can kill her three-year-old son in a safe, clean environment. You say, "That's stupid." You're right!

I beg you on behalf of that life developing within you, please don't get an abortion. If your womb only had that window, I know you would be amazed and overwhelmed at what a miracle life just beginning really is.

You say to me, "OK, Greg, then help me. What are the options?" Well, as I see it you really have three options:

☐ Keep the child, and raise it as a single parent.

To keep the child is a huge commitment. More often than not this needs to be a whole family decision, because, to be realistic, your parents will take a lot of that responsibility.

☐ Get married, and have the baby.

Now let me be honest and tell you that the odds are really against you. Better than 70 percent of teen marriages end in divorce. The younger you are, the harder it is. Then add the pressure of a new baby, and it will be very tough.

But if you're ready to stick to your vow "till death do us part," and if you're twenty now (remember, it's not unusual to live to be seventy), that means being married to the same person for fifty years. But if you're still determined, then get as much help and support from your families as possible. If your parents are against the marriage, then don't get married. I believe that God works through our parents for our good, whether they are Christian or not.

Then get yourself some good marriage counseling. The couples that ask me to marry them must meet with me about eight times for two hours per session. In addition, they have outside work to do.

☐ Let the child be adopted.

Many wonderful, godly couples can't have children and are praying for the chance to adopt. This would be a tremendous sacrifice, I know, but you would be thinking of the baby's well being above your own. Abortion leads to death and depression, but adoption leads to life and hope!

You're pregnant. It was a bad choice, but it's not the end of the world. Now let's make a good choice that's positive for everyone, especially the baby. What do you do?

☐ *You need to tell your parents.* "But my dad will kill me!" Are you sure? Think of other crises that have occurred and how your parents responded. You may be very surprised at how well they respond to this. When you tell your parents, you don't have to be alone. Have your pastor, youth pastor, adult friend, teacher, or friend go with you.

☐ *Get things straight with God.* He has never stopped loving you. As a prodigal daughter, come back home. His forgiveness is complete. There is tremendous hope for the future. Your life isn't doomed.

What were you before you became pregnant, and what did you want to become? Well, it's still possible, because you've got a great God. Just decide not to be involved sexually anymore so that the next time you're pregnant it will be with your husband.

☐ *Tell the boy and his parents.* It would be good if both families got together and talked it out. The boy needs to take on responsibility and at least bear some of the burden financially.

☐ *Go to your pastor and decide what steps should be taken within the Body of Christ.* It would be good to go before the church and confess. That way you have the Body of Christ coming to your support, and the problem's out in the open. You'll feel 110 percent better. And that's better than trying to sneak around or away.

☐ *Be patient with yourself.* You will go through several steps: denial, anger, fear, acceptance. This may take a while, but it will happen quicker if you are open and allow others to love and support you.

When you make the right decisions, you'll never regret them. Abortion is a horribly wrong decision you will live to regret.

Let me give you a twenty-four hour crisis pregnancy counseling hotline. If you are scared, alone, confused, pressured, call 1/800-238-4269. They will find you help, plus give you some solid answers to your questions. Tell them Greg Speck told you to call. It's toll free.

I have a good friend named Ruth who is a teenager. Ruth made a bad choice, and she became pregnant. I asked if she would write a letter about her experience that I could put in this book.

Thank you, Ruth, for caring enough to go through the heartache of putting this all down on paper for us. I know it's your prayer along with mine that this will be of help and encouragement to other teens.

Dear Greg,

This has been one of the hardest letters I've ever written. I've tried over and over to try to get things to come out "right," and they just haven't. Today I called a friend and explained to her that this was really getting to me. I knew I wanted to write, but it just wouldn't come together.

She gave me good advice. She told me to write from the heart. To forget all the big words and just write it as it comes out. "Let somebody else put the big words in for you later."

Well, that's what I'm going to try. Maybe this will all just be choppy and jumbled, and at this point I don't care if you even use it for your book. I just need to get it out as part of my own healing process. I realize that now.

I'm not sure why I had sex. Maybe it was the common "I don't really like myself" problem. Maybe I was "looking for love." Maybe I just wanted to please him because if I didn't, I'd lose my boyfriend, and having a boyfriend was the "in" thing.

Maybe it was just curiosity. Maybe it was rebellion because sex was "forbidden." Maybe it was peer pressure. Maybe it was all of those things together.

I know that he liked me. I liked him, and it felt good to be liked by someone. I don't say "loved," because I never really loved him, and I don't know if he loved me or not. Looking back now I don't think so, but I don't know what he felt for sure.

Whatever the reason was, we did have sex, and I know it was wrong. I knew it was wrong when it happened. I knew it was wrong long before it happened. I had even decided long ago that I would never have premarital sex, but I did. The guy I was dating was not a Christian, and I got farther away from God the longer we were going

together. I let my standards drop, and I rationalized myself into thinking it was OK just once and
nothing would ever happen.

In the back of my mind I knew once was all it
took to get pregnant, but I thought that would
never happen to me. I don't know why I thought I
was immune. I did get pregnant, and I told him
about it after I went to a clinic to find out for sure.
He was truly shocked and said, "I thought you
took care of that."

Greg, I hate it when it gets to this part, because now I know how precious life is and what a
miracle babies are, but I told him real casually, "I
will take care of it. I'll just get an abortion," like
it was the thing to do on your typical Saturday
afternoon.

He said he'd pay for everything. A couple
weeks later I told him I'd changed my mind, and I
wanted to have the baby. He told me I would ruin
his life and how he couldn't be a father now because his whole life was ahead of him and he was
finally graduating and going out into the real
world. He didn't speak to me after that.

I went through a lot of counseling, and God
worked on me a lot. I had the baby and placed her
for adoption.

It's been a year now since my baby was
born—her birthday was two days ago (three days
after mine). Now she's one year old. They tell me
she's walking and has six teeth. ("They" meaning
the adoptive parents.) She has curly hair—that's
from her father.

I miss her, Greg. I haven't cried for her in a
long time, but I am now—sorry if the pages get
wet.

Sometimes I cry out of happiness. From the
two letters I've received from her adoptive parents, I can tell they love her so much. They do
things with her. They're a real family. I could

never have given her that. Her dad reads to her, and she tries to turn the pages—she can't quite do that yet.

She calls them Mama and Daddy. I have mixed feelings about that. At first I was so happy for them. My first prayer is for her salvation, my second for them to grow together as a strong family—and they're doing that.

I want her to know that they are her family. They are her mom and dad, who will be there when she cuts herself or scrapes her knee or throws up all over her bedroom floor. They'll clean it up, not me. I want them to know she is their daughter.

I won't knock on their door someday and demand her back. I won't search for her and kidnap her from school, never to be heard from again. And so, I am happy that she calls them Mama and Daddy, and yet it hurts deep down where I try not to feel anything.

It doesn't hurt like it did before. I have no real regrets or bitterness. I have worked through that, and God has healed me, but it hurts in a different way to know that she'll call someone else Mom on Mother's Day. You have kids, Greg. You can understand.

By now I'm done crying—you see, I really am a lot better. I don't sob endlessly anymore because of missing her. Most of the time I remember the good times—the days in the hospital when I held her and fed her, the times when I saw her smile and sleep so peacefully, the friends I've made through my pregnancy, and the lessons I've learned. These are all good things that I remember.

This has been a really heavy duty letter, and it's not really book material. But it sure has made me feel a lot better.

I guess the thing I hate the most is the feeling that I could tell someone my whole story but it wouldn't mean anything unless they knew me. I mean I read books like yours, and I was stupid enough to do it anyway.

I had to learn from my own experience instead of someone else's. My dad says that real wisdom is being able to learn from someone else's mistakes rather than having to learn by making your own.

I don't mean this to be a "downer" about your book, Greg, because there are wise people out there who can learn from other people's mistakes —even mistakes of people they don't know. And for just one of them not to have sex, I'd write a whole book to send to you. I guess to one of those people I'd say, Don't have sex because . . .

Obviously you could get pregnant. Pregnancy is not fun for an unwed, confused, teenage girl. . . .

Well, Greg, it is 12:00 midnight, and I'm gonna call it quits. I feel a lot better. Thanks for being there for me, Greg—I love you. I pray for you often—don't forget that.

Love and prayers,
Ruth

8

Incest
(An Open Letter)

*"When I walk down the street I wonder if
people can see through me like a glass."* □

One out of ten boys and one out of four girls are victims of incest.

When I heard that statistic, I felt numb. I thought of you and others like you who struggle with this trying situation, feeling so alone, so misunderstood, so hopeless.

Not a spiritual retreat goes by but that, if I mention incest, at least two or three individuals come and talk with me. Then there are the letters from teens who have been suffering silently. Let me reproduce an excerpt from one letter I recently received.

> There are things in my life that are so confusing and so painful that I have just longed for my death, and I feel like this because I can't picture myself living life with a never ending feeling of agony. It is so very hard for me to wake up every morning and face the day. No, I will never take my own life, but I can't help but wish that someone would.
>
> Sometimes I will cry and cry, and I just feel so helpless. I don't know what to do. All I can think about is my brother and why, why would he, how could he? And, oh, it is so devastating,

117

and I am so empty inside, like I've been drained
and he took everything wonderful that I could
feel at this time in my life.

Such a feeling . . . of violation, and anguish,
and so much . . . anger. If he could step inside of
me and feel the pain in my heart and confusion in
my mind, it would drive him insane, absolutely
insane!

When I walk down the street I wonder if people can see through me like a glass. It scares me.
They shan't ever know. And my family . . . I want
and need so much to be held close, wrapped up as
secure as a cocoon, and [to] know that I am safe
from any more pain.

Of all the feelings I have ever known, it is my
loneliness and grief and personal tragedy that
hold me . . . in such a vicious grip I can not tell
you! . . .

Never before have I reached so deep into my
heart and pulled out all that makes me what I am
and shared this with anyone. I do not have to face
you, or be near you, or . . . see your reaction, so
this is not hard.

I shall hope that one day the battle that lies
within me . . . will come to rest so that I may heal
and become everything that God knows I am ca-
pable of becoming and the person I so desperately
desire to be!

Thank you for being such a friend.

Did your heart break as mine did when I read that
letter? I want to reach out, give this woman a hug, and
tell her there is hope. This chapter is for her and for
all of you who feel caught in the incest trap with no
way to escape.

I have a friend named Scott Harrison. He has
worked with incest victims, and I asked if he would be
willing to write a letter to you and share some insights.

Scott has done extensive counseling in this area, and he really does care about *you.*

Dear friend,

Hi. My name is Scott. I hope you don't mind reading this letter as a part of a book. I would much rather have sent it to you personally, but God has wonderful and sometimes unusual ways of bringing people and needed information together.

"But," you may be asking, "why a letter and not an ordinary chapter?"

Because incest is not an "ordinary" topic. An ordinary chapter would do if my purpose was to tell you how to choose a college or where to vacation in beautiful Colorado. But in writing about incest, the most personalized subject of all, an ordinary chapter won't do.

So even though this letter is part of a book, try to read it as it is intended—a personal letter to you from one you don't even know but one who cares very much about your healing.

I'd like to break the ice by venturing a guess as to what might be two ingredients of your thinking right now. I'm not writing to you as a fellow victim, so I can't say that I know exactly what you are thinking or how you feel. But through my research and counseling of others in similar circumstances, I have observed some common threads in thought patterns.

Please don't be offended if I mistakenly classify you as the so-called "typical" victim. I am well aware that you are one of a kind, simply because there is no one on this planet quite like you or the members of your family. You might say that God threw away the mold after creating each one of us.

My first guess at what might be a part of your thinking is what I refer to as "the cancer of confusion."

This "disease" is brought on by a series of unanswered questions—good questions like:

☐ What exactly is incest?
☐ Am I the only one?
☐ Why did it happen in our family?
☐ Why are my feelings so confused?
☐ Why not just forget it and go on?
☐ What can be done about it now?

The frustration of not having answers to these questions can cause the "cancer of confusion" to attack. It can eat away at the fiber of your being and drain you of all enthusiasm for living.

My second piece of guesswork goes hand in hand with the first. I call it "a fog of fear." In most situations the victims, as the rest of the family, have conditioned themselves to bury any thoughts of the incest in a pit of their minds labeled "top secret."

Sometimes the memory is buried so deeply in guilt that the victim has difficulty remembering all the details. The fear comes at the prospect of digging up these old memories, exposing "the family secret," and reliving the misery. Because of this mysterious "fog," you may hesitate to even read this letter, much less think about your own experience.

Can you see how your thinking can be totally paralyzed by these two ingredients? Your questions cry out to be answered, but your fears create such an emotional fog that you can't see the answers. The sad result is often an emotional wound that is never allowed to heal and is left wide open to infection.

This brings me to the main purpose for my writing. My goal is your healing. But in order for this to happen, your "cancer of confusion" must begin to be cleared up and your "fog of fear" must be courageously overcome.

To be honest, I can help you only with the first. I can only hope to clear up some of your confusion by answering that incomplete series of questions. My part is simply ink on a page. It is your part, the courage to face your fears, that will make the difference.

WHAT EXACTLY IS INCEST?

Simply stated, incest is any sexually arousing contact between family members. It may include prolonged kissing, fondling of breasts or genitals, mutual masturbation, oral sex, or actual intercourse. It makes no difference how long it went on or how innocent in nature it appeared. Any inappropriate sexual contact between family members is considered incestuous.

One way incest is often categorized is by the relationship involved. Although father-daughter incest is the most reported (75 percent), it is thought that brother-sister incest happens most frequently. Few of these cases get reported, however, since many times they involve sexual experimentation between children of similar ages and are usually not exploitive or psychologically damaging.

Though mothers are less likely to abuse children, there is a small percentage of mother-son incest. Other types include every imaginable family relationship including a mother's boyfriend.

Legally speaking, incest is a felony and can be punishable by a prison sentence. However, the goal of many newly instituted programs is not to jail anyone but to help the family back to health.

I'm sorry if these last three paragraphs were painful for you to read. I want to encourage you to read on anyway, in hopes of finding comfort for your pain.

AM I THE ONLY ONE?

Friend, there are two statements that are critically important for any incest victim to hear over and over again. The first is *You are not alone,* and the second is *It is not your fault.* Let me expand on the first. You may feel extremely alone emotionally, but there are literally millions of others who have gone through or are going through similar situations. The irony of it is that you may see each other every day and yet not know of your common bond. They may sit next to you in class or go to your church. No doubt you have talked with them. All the while both of you are pretending that everything is OK, and at the back of your minds each is saying, "If you only knew . . . "

Statistics are sometimes dry and difficult to grasp, but just imagine that one in every four of your girl friends will also be victims of some sort of sexual abuse before they leave home. In 75 to 85 percent of these cases, the abuser will be someone she knows and trusts, someone in the family or community.

I say "she" because about 90 percent of all incest victims are female. Conservative estimates say that well over 1 million American women have been involved in incestuous relationships with either their fathers or stepfathers. That is enough to equal the population of Houston, Texas, our nation's fifth largest city!

Not only are you not alone, but yours is not the only social class, economic level, race, religion, or neighborhood affected. Incest is no respecter of persons. It cuts through all such barriers, just as it has since Bible times. (Laws concerning incest go all the way back to Leviticus 18!)

No, you are definitely not alone. Many who are younger, many who are older, and thousands who are just your age are experiencing the same hell that you have lived in. Certainly that is a sad fact from which to draw comfort.

Why Did It Happen in Our Family?

Although it is helpful to know that you are not alone, it is far more important to hear the second statement that all victims need to know. If you forget every other word of this letter, don't forget these four: IT'S NOT YOUR FAULT!

Write them down, put them over your mirror, scribble them on the back of your wallet picture, write a song about them! How can I say with such confidence that it is not your fault? Because it is impossible for incest to *ever* be the child's fault!

Let me illustrate this very important point by telling you a parable.

One day a man walked into a nice restaurant to have dinner. The menu was filled with pictures of all their finest delectables. There was only one problem. The man's doctor had forbidden him to eat desserts. But he rationalized that he could make up for it tomorrow, and besides it had been a very stressful day. So after his meal he chose a piece of banana cream pie for dessert.

After he'd thoroughly enjoyed his first few bites, his conscience began to bother him. A second later he threw down his fork and screamed for all to hear, "It's the pie's fault!" He began to smash the pie with his fists, all the while complaining that the pie had caused him to go off his diet and get into trouble with his doctor.

Do you see the point of this silly illustration? Just as it is impossible for a piece of pie to be guilty of making anyone decide to go off a diet, it is also impossible

for an incest victim to be guilty of her abuser's decision to abuse her.

No matter how you rationalize that you may have "led him on" or in any way contributed to the occurrence, it is still your father's responsibility to decide and act.

As one victim capsulized it, "If they [the fathers] don't commit it [the incest], it doesn't happen." May I repeat, incest is not and cannot be the child's fault.

So why did the incest happen? This simple question can only be given a complex answer.

In most cases the incest is just the final large explosion of little "land mines" that had been ready to go off for quite some time. Some of these were set during the parent's own childhood. Many abusers were abused themselves as children. Thus they pass along to their children the only style of parenting they know.

However, not all abusing parents were victims. Many of the mines were set during the parent's marriage.

Little mines commonly found in both parents are low self-image, poor communication, little or no problem-solving skills, unrealistic marital expectations, and an inability to handle change or stress.

The father's mine field often includes being very authoritarian, extremely possessive, violent, and a substance abuser, lacking impulse control, and always in need of emotional fulfillment.

The mother is dotted with mines of extreme dependency, immaturity, and coldness in her relationship to her daughter. This "relational gap" is usually created through a role reversal, where the mother in effect becomes the little girl and the little girl is expected to fill her mother's shoes. As a whole, the family tends to isolate itself from the rest of society.

It is the combination of these many typical characteristics, or land mines, all exploding at once that blow the doors wide open for incest to occur. However, don't allow all this verbage to cause you to forget the main point. Even though a door is wide open, or the pie is on the menu, it is still the choice of the individual to walk through the door or eat the pie.

Moms and dads are the ones in charge in the family. It is up to them alone to make decisions as to which doors they walk through and which pies they eat.

In other words, IT'S NOT YOUR FAULT! Have you put those words to music yet? It will be the most beautiful song you'll ever hear.

WHY ARE MY FEELINGS SO CONFUSED?

My friend, it is with the same certainty that I told you it's not your fault, that I tell you that it's impossible for your feelings to be anything but confused. Why? Because, like dropping a quarter in a rigged slot machine and pulling the handle down, your emotions have been conditioned to be a mixture. Instead of seeing "Apples, Apples, Apples" ("love, love, love") pop up in the window, you might get "Apples, Oranges, Lemons" ("love, hate, embarrassment"). It's rare that you experience any unified emotions, because your "slot machine," your mind, has been trained to think in this jumbled fashion.

It can be a painful assignment to review your feelings in small clusters—much less to dump out the whole barrel at once. Yet I truly believe that your being willing to examine this conditioning process ever so briefly can be a great help to better understanding your confused feelings.

Look at all the times your emotional handle was pulled only to find a mixed result. The most confusing set of emotions stems from the thought *It must be right* because it's someone in authority who's initiating it. But at the same time you know *it must be wrong*, because of its secrecy. This confusion in itself is enough to blow up any emotional slot machine, but there are many more examples.

☐ You were looking for love but were made an object of lust.

☐ You were needing protection from the outside world but instead were abused by your inner circle.

☐ You were only a child but were treated as an adult. In most cases it felt good to have emotional needs met, but not in that way.

☐ You hated the act but at times could enjoy the power that it brought.

☐ Perhaps there was the enjoyment of natural physical sensations, yet the terrible guilt that came with it.

☐ There may have been the disgust of knowing a "public" dad and a "private" dad.

☐ The fear of becoming pregnant, yet the assurance that it couldn't or wouldn't happen.

☐ Wanting desperately to tell, yet facing the potential frustration and embarrassment of not being believed.

☐ Wanting to tell, yet feeling responsible for "holding the family together" by not telling.

☐ Wanting to tell, but not wanting to hurt Mom or possibly be hurt by Dad.

☐ Hoping and praying for things to change but living with cracked hopes and broken promises.

☐ Wanting to run away but not being old enough.

☐ Groping for support from Mom but getting a cold shoulder.

☐ Wanting the incest to stop with you but not wanting it to start with your siblings.

☐ Detesting your own family and being jealous of "normal" ones.

☐ Feeling in the pit of despair yet not allowing yourself to dwell on it.

☐ Looking for a true apology but getting only a series of rationalizations.

☐ Trying hard to forget but interrupted so often by flashbacks or nightmares.

☐ Wanting to find help but not believing anything can really be done.

☐ Searching for healthy relationships but feeling unable, "already used" and unclean.

☐ Wanting to scream, but nothing coming out; to cry, but no tears to be found; to die, but your heart keeps pumping.

The bottom line is that no one can go through such a mixture of experiences and then pull her emotional handle and expect to see beautifully unified emotions pop up in the window. The value in knowing this is that it keeps you from thinking you are some kind of emotional freak. Mixed-up emotions are actually the norm.

As a matter of fact, the degree of emotional confusion can be directly related to the type of incest, the length of the incestuous period, your age at the time, and the amount of treatment you have already received.

The good news is that your emotional slot machine can be reprogrammed. The sad news is that if the reality of emotional confusion is never faced, emotional healing will never come.

WHY NOT JUST FORGET IT AND GO ON?

There are two good reasons why you can't just forget about the incest and go on with life.

The first is probably obvious to you from your own experience. You simply can't forget. It's just not possible. It would be like trying to forget your name. It simply becomes part of who you are. Though this is difficult to accept, you must understand this truth: you will always be a victim—a "triumphant survivor," hopefully, but always a victim.

The second reason you can't just forget and go on is that you bear what one victim calls the "invisible scars" that become the trademark of incest victims. These scars make it impossible to forget.

No doubt the ugliest scar of all is that of a poor self-image. This is brought on by a tremendous sense of guilt for having been involved in something that was against your conscience. Even though it is false guilt (since incest is never the fault of the child), it is close enough to the real thing to become a terrible emotional weight, and it robs you of any sense of self-worth.

So your mind sends a message to your heart in bright, flashing neon lights: "You're no good and are of no use to anyone." The message is then translated into several different languages and sent throughout your life.

The message can be translated into social terms and stimulate a desire to run away or to marry at an early age. It can cause difficulty in forming intimate relationships or possibly lead one to become a prostitute. (One study of adolescent female prostitutes found that 75 percent had been victims of incest.) Translated into emotional language, it often results in deep depression and even suicide.

Translation into the physical realm can take the form of excessive drinking or drug abuse. Still another translation into the practical aspect of living is reflected in sleep disturbances, sexual dysfunctions, and of course the sad prospect of passing on the message to the next generation.

But no matter what the translation, the results are always destructive, because false guilt can produce no good thing.

Although the incest can never be forgotten, some victims still try to cope by "just ignoring it." Some develop creative techniques like never sitting still long enough to think, stubbornly denying it ever happened, or even focusing all their energies on solving others' problems. All are diligent exercises in futility. Sooner or later the make-up wears off, and the ugly scars are exposed.

This is why you just can't forget it and go on.

WHAT CAN BE DONE ABOUT IT NOW?

For most victims the words, "What can be done about it now?" are not asked as a sincere question but rather as a hopeless declaration. I trust that you don't fit into this category, because it is this kind of attitude that keeps most "victims" from ever becoming "triumphant survivors."

They get caught in the trap of only thinking of the act of incest itself. They say, "It's over now, and besides you can't change the fact that it happened." That's right, you can't change the past, but you can stop the past from ruining your present future!

Dear friend, your future is full of hope as bright as the sun that lights a cloudless sky at noonday. It is spectacular in its beauty!

Those words may sound like a new language to you right now, and there's good reason for that. You must understand that you are locked up in a sort of emotional basement. You're hidden from the sunlight of hope.

That's why you need someone from the outside to describe it to you and lead you out of the basement so that you can see it for yourself. That's been my purpose in writing you this letter. I've tried to sit with you in your cellar and answer some of your questions.

Now I need to give you some specific directions on how to get out of the basement. *There is a way out!* Women all around you are stepping from darkness into the bright light of hope every day. On the other hand many seem content to sit on a pile of emotional garbage in their lifeless basements.

As much as I would like to pick you up and carry you out, I can't. The choice has to be yours. You must get up and walk on your own. If you are willing, and I pray that you are, there are three steps you must

climb to get out of the basement. It won't be the easiest thing you've ever done, but it will be the best.

☐ *The first step has to do with assigning guilt where true guilt belongs.*

Every incest victim is confronted with two major options of where to assign guilt. You may either lay it at the feet of the abuser or keep it for yourself. Since most choose the second option, a "guilt transfer" needs to take place. By this I mean that you must transfer your self-condemnation to the one worthy of it: the abuser.

Don't misunderstand me. I'm not asking you to disown your father or even to throw darts at his picture. I'm saying that your healing won't begin until you understand that it is the abuser's responsibility, not yours.

You'll know that this transfer has been accomplished when you can honestly say, "I truly believe that the incest was not my fault at all."

☐ *The second step has to do with granting forgiveness to your abuser.*

You see, the purpose of transferring the guilt is not to transfer hate. That would only add to your problems. Rather, the purpose of the transfer is to free you from hating yourself. These steps are designed for your healing. However, if you choose to carry the guilt —or the hate—on your own shoulders, you'll not have any energy to give to the healing process.

You'll know you've taken this step when you can say to your abuser, "I understand that what you did to me was wrong, but by the grace of God I forgive you." (If your abuser is no longer living, you may simply write him a letter to this effect, sign it, and then burn it.)

☐ *The third step has to do with the emotional bandaging of those invisible wounds before they become permanent scars.*

Though the most important of these were dealt with in steps one and two, others need attending to. Wounds such as low self-esteem, nonassertiveness, sexual dysfunctioning, distrust of men, poor communication skills, flashbacks, depression. One dear victim called these her "post-graduate courses." Working through these issues will enable you to deal with the everyday struggles without these added "wounds" draining your energy before you can get started. As this "graduate level" victim put it, her glimpses of hope are getting closer together all the time.

When you can say that, you'll know you are accomplishing the third step.

I need to add two short notes.

First, these steps can't be taken overnight—or in any shortcut fashion. Remember, any cost for your total healing is worth it.

Second, you shouldn't take these steps alone. You'll need an outsider who knows how to deal with incest specifically. This toll-free number can put you in touch with people in your area who will assist you in finding help: 800/422-4453. I, too, would very much like to be of any help I can. My address is:

Scott Harrison
1601 S. Oak St.
Bloomington, IL 61701

My friend, I have shared with you some strong statements concerning incest. I have said that you are not alone, that it is not your fault, that it is natural to have confused feelings, that you can't just forget about it, and that there is hope and healing.

In closing, I must add one more. God loves you. He loves you just the way you are. There is nothing you can do to make Him love you any more or any less. He loves you so much that He was willing to send His only Son to die on the cross in your place.

Have you responded to His love for you? If you haven't, trust Him to be your Savior today.

Rejoicing in the bright light of His hope,
Your friend Scott

9

Rape
(Why It Happens and What to Do)

When you aren't prepared, then the
chances of rape greatly increase. ☐

Ask a woman, "What's one of the worst things that could happen to you?" and more often than not, she will say rape. Many, many women are terrified by the thought of being raped, and my wife is no exception.

Most of us don't want to talk about rape, because it is such an ugly subject. But we have to talk about it. It may happen to us or to someone we know. Each year more than 80,000 women report being raped, but it's estimated that more than 900,000 never report the attack. And this in one year! Also we are seeing an increase in the number of men being raped by other men.

If you deny that rape could ever happen to you, then you are not preparing yourself for the possibility. When you aren't prepared, then the chances of rape greatly increase.

WHO MIGHT RAPE ME?

The mental picture we have is of a dirty, gross individual who hides in alleys, ready to grab a victim. Yes, those people exist, but do you realize that more than 50 percent of those raped know the person who is doing this?

For example, you need to be aware of date rape. Girls are being raped by the very men who are taking them out.

Certain men will feel justified in forcing you to have intercourse with them if any one of these four things has occurred:

☐ If you excited him. (We have already learned that men tend to be visually oriented. You could have excited him by just walking to the car.)
☐ If he feels you have been leading him on.
☐ If you have previously messed around a little.
☐ If you said yes but later changed your mind.

Understand that, from the man's point of view, he may not consider this rape. He may feel that if anyone is at fault, it's you!

That says to me that you better know the person you are dating. Bonnie and I have a friend named Nancy. She says she would be insulted if a guy just called her on the phone and asked her out and she didn't really know him. Why? Because obviously all he was attracted to was her body and face.

Let me make some suggestions that will certainly lessen the likelihood of being attacked.

☐ *Date only Christians.*
   I can hear it now, "But there are hardly any Christians around me, and those I do know remind me of the Three Stooges!" Look, you have trusted Jesus Christ with your eternity, so you can trust Him with your dating life. He knows your needs better than even you know. So don't just talk about trusting Jesus—trust Him.

☐ *Be friends first.*

Get to know him before you go out with him. Invite him over to your house, and let him meet your parents. He is less likely to attack you if he has developed a relationship with your parents.

☐ *Don't date alone.*

Go out on group dates, or at least double-date. That way you'll have other individuals around to assist you. It's always better to be safe.

WHY DO THEY WANT TO RAPE ME?

Most men do not rape for sexual reasons. They rape because . . .

☐ They want to feel important. They may have a poor self-image, feelings of inferiority, and to rape a woman means that they are significant.

☐ They may be angry. Angry at their mother or sisters. Maybe angry because of some embarrassment they have experienced at the hands of a woman, so they are getting even.

☐ They want to be in control. They have been dominated in the past, and this is their opportunity to dominate someone else.

☐ They want to inflict pain. There are sadistic individuals who derive pleasure from hurting someone else.

☐ They want to belong. In the case of gang rape, they can be accepted by the group. If they didn't rape, they might be rejected.

When you understand some of the reasons for rape, you discover that rape is not sexual primarily but rather is an act of violence. There are few similarities between rape and sexual intercourse in a loving marriage relationship.

Realize that a rapist is most often looking for a woman who is weak and vulnerable. So in a dating situation, be firm. Don't try to be kind. "Well, I don't want to hurt his feelings." Women have told me that. Go ahead and hurt his feelings, because he is seeking to hurt more than your feelings.

If he senses that you are unsure, confused, or fearful, he may try to take advantage of you. Remember that any man who tries to rape you is certainly not in love with you.

WHERE DOES RAPE USUALLY OCCUR?

The three most likely places for a rape situation would be . . .

☐ Your own house or apartment
☐ A car
☐ His house or apartment

You see, for a man to rape you, he needs to somehow get you isolated. So you don't want to let that happen.

Don't park with him. Don't get caught at each other's place when nobody is home. Here are some other suggestions.

☐ Whatever you do, don't hitchhike. You don't know who is going to pick you up.
☐ When traveling alone, always check the backseat of the car before you get in.
☐ If you're outside at night, stay in lighted places. Don't take shortcuts through dark, isolated areas like alleys and parks.
☐ If you sense you are being followed, go to a public place and call the police. Don't go home if you are being followed, because he will then know where you live.

In other words, be careful. Don't set yourself up to be raped.

WHAT SHOULD I DO IF I AM ATTACKED?

I wish I could tell you one thing to do that always works if you are attacked. But I can't. Each rapist is different, and each is raping for different reasons. What works for one person may not work for another. I can give you six possible options. I'm sure there are more, but at least these will give you some alternatives.

Before I list these, please know that it's important you stay as calm as possible. Now I know that's easy for me to say, but I say it for two reasons. First, if you panic, the chances are that you will excite him. You will be meeting his expectations. He knows that a weak and vulnerable woman will react that way. But if you can remain calm, that communicates strength to him.

And second, you've got to think, and you won't be able to do that if you're out of control emotionally.

So what are some options?

☐ *Pray out loud.*

Ask God to protect you and make His presence known. Pray for your attacker and for his soul. Quote Scripture that you have memorized. The Word of God is powerful and sharper than any two-edged sword. There is a good possibility that the rape is demonically inspired. In that case prayer and the Word of God are your best weapons.

☐ *Be personal.*
Tell him some things about yourself so that he can see you as some*body* and not some*thing*. Show some concern for him. There are probably areas in his life that he is struggling with. You want him to see you as more than just an object. Calling him terrible names will just make him angrier.

☐ *Be gross.* Stick your finger down your throat and throw up all over yourself. Pick your nose. Put the mucus on your face, or eat it. Urinate on yourself and wherever you are. Cause some concern and confusion on his part by asking him questions like . . .

- Have you ever had herpes?
- Do you want to get AIDS?
- Does it matter to you if I have a sexually transmitted disease?
- You want to do this if I'm having my period?

You want to seek to be disgusting and to do things that will make you less attractive to him.

☐ *Be bizarre.*
Pretend you have snapped mentally. Act strangely.

☐ *Play along.*
You could momentarily play along, as though this is something you enjoy and want. You are doing this so that he will relax, let down his guard, loosen his grip, and you can escape. But it's important that you have somewhere to escape to. If he has isolated you, if you're parked out in the middle of nowhere, then this won't work.

(Remember that in the above scenarios you are for all intents and purposes an actress, and you had better be good. If he senses that you are trying to trick him, he can become even more hostile.)

☐ *Counterattack.*

You can try physical violence yourself. But if you decide to do this, you are going to have to really hurt him. He has got to be stunned long enough for you to get away. Again this won't work if you have nowhere to run.

Take a sharp object—pencil, pen, key, nail file, scissors, tweezers—and jam it as hard as you can into his eye. I guarantee this will immediately stop the rape. Or grab his testicles and squeeze hard. If you do this as hard as you can, he will experience tremendous pain. The rape attempt will stop, and you should have a few moments to get away. But it's important that you don't just lie there. Push or kick him out of the way and get out of there.

I warn you that you are taking a tremendous risk. If you fail to hurt him enough to get away, he can do terrible damage to you. Thus it boils down to whoever is the more violent wins, and that will usually be the man.

You stand a much better chance if you have had some training in self-defense. Even with that, it's going to be very difficult. When prisoners in jail for rape were asked what they would do if a woman fought back, about 50 percent said they would let her go. But the other 50 percent would have got even tougher.

I suggest you take this step if you believe your attacker is going to kill you. At that point you really have nothing to lose.

How Do I Know If I've Made the Right Choice?

If you're alive, you've made the right choice. Many women never live through this ordeal.

What Do I Do If I'm Raped?

□ *Get to a safe place.*

If you're with him in the car, promise anything as long as you can leave. Go to a gas station, restaurant, market, anywhere there there are people, so that you can get some protection.

□ *Get some support.*

Call someone to come to be with you right now, perhaps your parents. They will certainly need to know. Or call your youth pastor, pastor, friend. Don't go through the next several hours alone.

□ *Call the police.*

They must be notified. If possible we need to catch this guy. You don't want him to do this to some other girl and have her go through what you're going through now.

But don't touch anything. Don't wash, comb your hair, brush your teeth, change your clothes, or anything else. Without knowing, you may be destroying important evidence. You'll desperately want to shower, but don't!

I am one of the chaplains for the Rockford, Illinois, Police Department, and we have been trained in this area. Police are making an effort to be sensitive and kind to someone who has gone through this ordeal.

□ *Go to the hospital.*

Go even if you don't think you need to. Most women are in shock at this point, and you really do need to be checked out. If for nothing else they want to make sure you haven't picked up any disease or infection, and they want to gather evidence in case you want to prosecute.

□ *Get some counseling.*

You're going to need some help in the days and weeks to come. You will feel so much better if there is someone who can not only weep with you but also help you sort through the emotions.

☐ *Allow others to serve you.*

One attitude of a servant of Christ is that of allowing others to serve you. You need to surround yourself with family and friends who will continue to just love you with unconditional love.

☐ *Be patient with yourself.*

It's going to take time, but, yes, you can recover. Be patient with yourself, because recovery usually doesn't happen overnight.

I want you to know that I get very angry at men who do this. Let me in conclusion mention two facts for you who have already been raped.

☐ This is not your shame but rather the shame of the one who did this terrible thing to you. Even though you may have led him on, dressed seductively, teased him, and got yourself into a stupid situation, a man never has the right to force himself on you. Rape is never justified.

☐ You are still a virgin. "What? How can you say that, Greg?" Because no one can take your virginity. That is something you freely give. The same is true of a victim of incest.

My prayer is that none of you will ever have to experience rape, although many already have. But at the same time I must stress the importance of being prepared. Think ahead. Be aware, so that if it does come you'll be better able to deal with the situation. Better yet, you'll know how to avoid it altogether.

10

Masturbation
(Why Doesn't Anybody Talk About It?)

Many of us have listened to Satan's lies and actually don't believe we can ever have self-control in this area. That just is not true. □

Certain things strike fear into our individual hearts. For a swimmer it's the word *shark*. For a dieter it's, "Hey, anyone here want a hot fudge sundae?" For a student it's, "Clear your desk for a surprise quiz." For you who are going out on your very first date, it's a zit! And for the Christian seeking to lead a pure life, it's the word *masturbation.*

The word itself causes a variety of reactions: embarrassment, anger, guilt, shock, disgust. Why is it that masturbation causes such a stir among Christians?

There may be a lot of reasons, but let me suggest one. I believe masturbation evokes such responses because the problem is so personal and it affects so many of us.

Now you can find statistics to support just about anything you want to talk about. But conservative statistics today would say that 90 percent of males and 50 percent of females have participated in masturbation. That means that some of your fathers, mothers, and even pastors have struggled with this question while growing up. To be perfectly honest, some of them continue to struggle with it.

You see, it's very difficult for people to talk about masturbation because so many of us have participated in it. But I believe we need to discuss it openly and honestly, and that we should view it from a Christian perspective.

What is masturbation? It is stimulating one's own genital organs to bring about orgasm, or sexual climax.

You will find a wide range of opinions concerning masturbation. Some people who will tell you that it is God's gift and that you should enjoy it. Others say masturbation is absolutely a sin and an abomination in God's sight.

One reason for such diversity of opinion is that God's Word is silent on the matter. Certain verses relate somewhat to masturbation, but God in no place mentions it specifically. As a result, everybody formulates his own opinion.

I agree with Dr. James Dobson that masturbation can be very harmful if it is followed by feelings of extreme guilt. But I see it as *sinful* if any one of the following develops:

☐ If the masturbation occurs in groups. This can easily lead to homosexual involvement.

☐ If the masturbation continues after marriage. You then are cheating your spouse. Instead of focusing your sexual energy on your wife or husband, you focus on yourself and your private fantasies. In addition, many times the person you imagine yourself to be with sexually is not your spouse.

☐ If the masturbation is done in conjunction with lusting and/or pornographic material. Colossians 3:17 says, "*Whatever* you do, whether in word or

deed, do it all in the name of the Lord Jesus, giving thanks to God the Father through him" (italics added).
☐ If the masturbation begins to control you, rather than your controlling it.
And that can happen. Masturbation can become a habit. We may use it to release stress, to fall asleep at night, as a reward for accomplishments, or as an escape from loneliness. The lust of the flesh takes control.

Check out these two Bible verses, and see how they tie into what I've just said:

☐ "They promise them freedom, while they themselves are slaves of depravity—for a man is a slave to whatever has mastered him" (2 Peter 2:19).
☐ "It is God's will that you should be sanctified [set aside for God's use]: that you should avoid sexual immorality; that each of you should learn to control his own body in a way that is holy and honorable, not in passionate lust like the heathen, who do not know God."

People tell me that they masturbate to relieve sexual tension. The sad fact is that masturbation usually does not relieve sexual tension. In the long run it causes even more tension. You see, the more you masturbate the more you want to masturbate. Often masturbation becomes an obsession. It grips you with such force that you lose all control.
Many of us have listened to Satan's lies and actually don't believe we can ever have self-control in this area. That just is not true. Too many of us interpret 1 Corinthians 10:13 this way: "No temptation has seized you except what is common to man. And God is faithful; he will not let you be tempted beyond what

you can bear [except when it comes to masturbation].
But when you are tempted, he will also provide a way
out so that you can stand up under it [except for mas-
turbation]."

We spend more time thinking about masturbation
than we do thinking about Jesus Christ. And when we
take our eyes off the person of Jesus Christ in the
midst of testing, that's when we get into trouble.

Look at Peter: He was sitting in a boat, safe and
secure, when he saw Jesus Christ walking on the water. Peter, who suffered from a terminal case of ath-
lete's mouth, opened it again, removed his left foot,
and put in his right foot by saying, "Well, if it is You,
Jesus, tell me to get out of the boat and come to You."
So Jesus said, "Come along, Peter."

Peter stepped out of the boat and began to walk.
He kept his eyes right on Jesus Christ, and he said to
himself, "Oh boy, I'm walking on water. Oh boy, I'm
walking on water!— What am I doing out here walking on water!"

And then he made a serious mistake. Peter took
his eyes off Jesus Christ and began to focus on the situation around him—the waves, the stormy clouds, the
raging wind—and now began to say to himself, "Hey,
listen, nobody ought to be out here just walking on the
water!"

And what happened to Peter? He began to sink.
Then there is recorded one of the most sincere prayers
ever uttered by any individual. As that cold, cold water began to creep up Peter's body, he focused back on
the person of Jesus Christ and uttered this profoundly
theological prayer, "Help!" Jesus lifted him up and put
him back in the boat.

Too many of us have taken our eyes off Jesus
Christ. We have focused on the masturbation. We
have failed so often that we have said to ourselves,

"There is no hope—I can never have self-control." As a result we have sunk into all of the garbage, the rubbish, and the lies that Satan would feed us.

Instead, let's turn our focus back to Jesus Christ. Let's call out for help. Let's allow Him to lift us above our circumstances and empower us to deal with this problem.

Masturbation never really satisfies. It's important to understand that one of the purposes of sex is to end loneliness. In the marriage relationship, sex between two people is a form of communication. And that is one reason masturbation never ever really satisfies. Masturbation is lust directed toward ourselves rather than love directed toward another person.

Down through the years, people have thought that the best way to counsel a young person about masturbation is to frighten him. Here are some of the

things that people used to say would happen if you masturbate.

- [ ] You will grow hair on your palms.
- [ ] You will eventually become impotent.
- [ ] You will go insane.
- [ ] You will develop warts.
- [ ] You will lose your sex organ.
- [ ] You will become blind.
- [ ] You will become gay.
- [ ] You will develop acne.
- [ ] Your growth will be stunted.
- [ ] Dark circles will form around your eyes.

The truth is that none of these things will occur if you masturbate, and the answer is found not in frightening someone but in giving wise advice. (If you try to frighten someone, the usual result is that the person will hide his habit instead of dealing with it.)

If you are caught in the cycle of masturbation, you need to know that there are individuals who have gained victory over this problem. Have confidence that God can also give you victory.

What are some things a person can begin to do to gain victory over masturbation? Let me give you some suggestions:

FACE IT

Stop avoiding or rationalizing the problem. Some of us try to pretend that the problem isn't there. We think that by ignoring it somehow it will just go away. But that isn't true, and you've already discovered that, so let's stop playing those games.

We need to face the fact that too often we are merely people who seek to do what feels good. We would rather masturbate, and gain pleasure for the moment, than serve Jesus Christ and gain a much greater satisfaction in the long run. Romans 13:14 says, "Rather, clothe yourself with the Lord Jesus Christ, and do not think about how to gratify the desires of the sinful nature."

It's important that you deal with masturbation now. Some have thought that as soon as they get married they will never again be tempted to masturbate. That simply is not true. After the newness of marriage has worn off, if you have masturbated or fantasized in the past, there is a strong possibility that you will continue after marriage. And you will probably be fantasizing about someone other than your partner.

PRAY SPECIFICALLY

Go to God, and ask Him for strength to begin to practice self-control.

Name the problem. Don't beat around the bush. God knows what you are struggling with, so tell Him that you need His help in the area of masturbation. But don't make promises!

Here is what we will typically do. We'll say to God, "Oh, God, I'm so sorry, but if you'll just forgive me one more time I promise I will never do it again."

Well, to be realistic, what happens? We do it again. Then what happens? We've made a promise to God, and guilt sets in. Satan laughs at us, and we feel totally out of fellowship with Him. Some people give up on their relationship with Christ because they cannot gain victory over the masturbation habit. Don't make promises.

EVALUATE WHAT YOU ARE TAKING INTO YOUR MIND

What kind of magazines, books, TV programs, and films are you reading and watching? What kind of music are you listening to? All these things are having an effect on you.

If you are struggling with masturbation and continue to sit watching sexual activity on the TV, you are only adding to your problem. Your standard for anything you take into your life ought to be Philippians 4:8:

> Finally, brothers, whatever is true, whatever is noble, whatever is right, whatever is pure, whatever is lovely, whatever is admirable—if anything is excellent or praiseworthy—think about such things.

Let me tell you openly and honestly that one of the worst things you can take into your mind is music videos. Now I know that is not going to endear me to many of you, but if you watch music videos on a regular basis, take pen and paper and list three categories: sex, violence, and spirit occult-type activities.

Then, as you watch, write down the name of each video and the name of the performer. If you see any sexual content, or violence, or spiritistic activity, put a check by the proper category. Do you know what you are going to discover? You are going to discover that music videos have an incredible amount of these, especially sexual content.

FILL YOUR MIND WITH WHAT IS POSITIVE

We should want to be pleasing, acceptable, and pure in God's sight.

> Romans 12:1—"Therefore, I urge you, brothers, in view of God's mercy, to offer yourselves as living sacrifices, holy and pleasing to God—this is your spiritual act of worship."

There's no getting around it. You need to spend time in the Word of God. The Bible is to your spiritual growth what food is to your physical growth. If you do not eat for a while you are not going to feel too good. If you do not dine spiritually for a while, you're not going to feel good spiritually.

You also need to be on your knees in prayer. A lack of communication indicates a lack of love, because you naturally communicate with one you love. When's the last time you and God have really done some communicating?

Begin to listen to Christian music. There is excellent contemporary Christian music out today. Plug into that.

Be careful about the friends you hang around with, because they are going to have an impact on your life. Remember 1 Corinthians 15:33: "Do not be misled: Bad company corrupts good character."

Memorize Scripture. Fill your mind with what is good and what is positive, and guess what? That's exactly what is going to come out of your life. Galatians 5:16: "So I say, live by the Spirit, and you will not gratify the desires of the sinful nature."

NOTE YOUR MASTURBATION PATTERN AND BREAK IT

Masturbation often has a pattern. For example, your alarm goes off at 6:30 in the morning, but you don't have to get up until 7:00. So what happens? You lie there, and fantasize, and eventually masturbate.

Or you come home from school, and the first thing you do is go into the bathroom (you've been waiting to go to the bathroom since third hour, so it's a priority). While looking through the magazines, you find pictures that excite you or stimulate your imagination, and that's when you masturbate.

Remember, masturbation becomes sinful when it is performed in conjunction with pornographic material. An example of that is found in Matthew 5:28, which warns against looking on a woman and lusting after her. When you do that, Jesus says, you commit adultery.

Or it happens before you fall asleep at night.

Notice when it usually occurs, and try to break the pattern.

That means setting your alarm for 7:00 A.M. When it goes off, get up and get ready for school. Or when you come home from school, don't grab a magazine—grab your Bible and go into the bathroom and read some Scripture. Or if you find it difficult to fall asleep at night, do a little reading. Do some praying, and really ask God to be in control of your thought life at that time. Meditate on Scripture. Begin to break out of the pattern of masturbation that is so controlling.

You may also notice an emotional pattern. You may find that when you are under a lot of pressure that's when it happens. You masturbate to gain a pleasurable release. You need to come up with some creative substitutes to cope with pressure. Get involved with people and activities that generate joy for you.

Second Timothy 2:22 says, "Flee the evil desires of youth, and pursue righteousness, faith, love and peace, with those who call on the Lord out of a pure heart."

PUT YOUR INTELLECT BACK IN CONTROL

When you masturbate, your emotions are in control of your intellect, and that isn't good.

If you are a smoker, you know that smoking is not necessary and that there are two ways you can try to quit smoking. One is to break cold turkey. Now some people can do that and be successful, but not everybody. The second way is to cut down the number of cigarettes you smoke until you eventually get down to where you are smoking so few cigarettes that it's much easier to stop.

Yes, some of us will be able to stop cold turkey. God will give these people victory immediately, and they will never ever have to masturbate again. But others of us are going to need to cut back on the frequency of the habit, doing it less and less, until we will eventually find that it will be much easier to stop.

What I want us to begin to do is to let our intellect control our emotions. Next time you are tempted to masturbate, I want you to ask yourself, "Is this necessary?" If the answer is no, then don't do it! Do you know what you are going to find immediately? The frequency of the masturbation will be cut back.

Understand that you don't have to masturbate. You have a choice. If you don't masturbate, nothing terrible is going to happen to you. You're not going to blow up or turn green. Your toes won't fall off. And as you see some victory in this area, as you see the frequency of the masturbation being cut back, that will give you the encouragement and the courage—along with Christ's power—to eventually stop.

GET A NEW PERSPECTIVE ON THE OPPOSITE SEX

Realize that men and women are creations of God. Each is, or at least potentially is, your brother or sister in Christ. Not only is it unhealthy for you to lust after another and to masturbate, but it is also unhealthy for the other person. When you masturbate, you are not looking at the person as somebody. You are merely looking at him or her as something.

Now I understand that when a woman mastur-
bates she is not always thinking about a sexual encounter. A woman may just be thinking of being held
or cared about. But, again, I do not believe that masturbation is the best thing we can be doing with our
bodies.

Men, let's remember Job 31:1: "I have made a covenant with my eyes not to look lustfully at a girl." I
mentioned this earlier, but let me remind you again
—when you are talking to a woman, always make eye
contact with her. Women have told me how degrading
it feels when they talk to a man and his eyes are moving up and down their bodies. That is a sign of disre-
spect.

Let's begin to see the opposite sex not as objects of
our desire but as our brothers or sisters in Christ, to be
respected, protected, and loved.

UNDERSTAND THAT WE ARE IN A BATTLE

Let's get in the fight. The following is an effective
way to combat Satan and his attacks in the area of
masturbation. We need to arm ourselves (Ephesians
6:13-18) with the . . .

☐ Belt of truth.
   This holds the rest of the armor together. You
need to be a man or woman of integrity. Have a
clear conscience. Always tell the truth. If your
word doesn't mean anything, then *you* don't mean
anything, because you are your word.
☐ Breastplate of righteousness.
   Live a godly life by the power of the Holy Spirit.
The life we live either fortifies us against Satan's
attacks or makes it easier for us to be defeated.
There is a war going on inside between our old and

new natures. Which one wins? Whichever one you feed the most!

☐ Shoes of the gospel.

Take the initiative. Talk about Jesus Christ in the power of the Holy Spirit, then leave the results to God. We tell of Christ in deed as well as word. By our actions we are either drawing people closer to Christ or pushing them farther away.

☐ Shield of faith.

Trust in the power and promises of Christ. When Satan attacks, claim those promises and resist him (1 Peter 5:9).

☐ Helmet of salvation.

Let your mind be controlled by God. Study and know the Word of God.

☐ Sword of the Spirit.

Use the Word of God to rebuke Satan in the name

of the Lord Jesus Christ. It's important that we *memorize* Scripture. Otherwise, if Satan attacks when we have no Bible handy, we could be in big trouble, just like a soldier caught without his weapon.

Now that's as far as people usually go when talking about putting on the full armor of God. Then I heard about a seventh piece! I am really excited about this one. It works. I know, because I've tried it. It is . . .

☐ Prayer in the Spirit.
"Pray in the Spirit," Ephesians 6:18 says. We are to use prayer as a defensive weapon every time we feel tempted by Satan. This is what you can do:

1.   Think of one non-Christian who, if he became a Christian, could do tremendous damage to Satan.
2.   Think of one Christian who is apathetic spiritually but who, if he came alive, would be a blow to the devil's kingdom.
3.   Think of some leaders in government.

Now, anytime you are tempted to masturbate, or for that matter are tempted in any area, I want you to pray for these individuals. You will discover that the temptation will weaken or stop altogether.
Why?
Because now you are advancing into Satan's very territory by praying for individuals he is controlling. He will feel that attack, and he will flee from you. Again why? Because of the tremendous power there is in prayer. Satan doesn't want to risk losing any of the people he controls. Satan can tolerate a lot of things that Christians do, but he hates our praying. So pray

without ceasing, and let's attack him at his very heart. Remember that the war is already won. We are just fighting some closing battles, so let's stop acting like losers.

TALK WITH SOMEONE

Talking with someone else about your problem is perhaps one of the most difficult steps to take. But find somebody whom you respect and whom you can trust. Men go to men, and women go to women. Find somebody who is older and wiser than yourself. Sit down with this person and tell about the struggle that you are having.

The more we withdraw and hide, the more likely we are to masturbate. Everything seems to be bigger and worse and more terrifying when it's hidden in the dark. After we see it in the light of day, it really isn't as bad as it seemed. Let's bring masturbation out in the light of day and get it back into perspective. Confide with somebody openly and honestly, and get the help, support, and care you need to begin to deal with it.

You'll have somebody who will be praying with you and for you that God will give you victory. And, second, you'll have someone to whom you can be accountable. That means periodically he can come up to you and say, "How are you doing? How's the battle going?" And you'll always know that somebody is going to be checking up on you. That can be an encouragement not to give up but to hang in there and do battle.

Remember the statistics: more than 90 percent of the men and more than 50 percent of the females. A lot of us have been involved in masturbation. We'll be able to identify with you and the struggle you are going through.

GET INVOLVED IN SERVICE AGAIN

Get involved in service again. Too often we do desire to follow Jesus Christ, but because we are struggling with masturbation we don't think that He can use us. So we take 90 percent of our energy and concentrate it on this one struggle. We stop growing, we become ineffective, and we no longer serve the Lord. How stupid is that? If we couldn't serve Jesus Christ until we were perfect, guess what? None of us would be serving, because we all struggle—just in different areas.

If you could be perfect, Christ would never have had to die for you. So put your eyes back on Jesus Christ, and allow Him to fill you with His Spirit.

1 Timothy 4:12 says, "Don't let anyone look down on you because you are young, but set an example for the believers in speech, in life, in love, in faith and in purity."

In spite of the fact that you are struggling in the area of masturbation, God can and will use you. Let Him.

BE PATIENT WITH YOURSELF

God is patient with you. You need to be patient with yourself.

In dealing with masturbation, it's really important that you relax. Many of you are so uptight that your tension just adds to the problem. Relax. Don't make the problem bigger or worse than it really is. When you fail, don't give up, don't toss in the towel. Get back up and keep going. It took you some time to get involved in masturbation. It will probably take you some time to gain victory over it.

Don't heap condemnation on yourself. Most of us are tougher on ourselves than anyone else would be on us. But we do have our priorities messed up if we spend more time masturbating than we do worshiping and serving Jesus Christ. Be patient; work on your priorities, and don't give up! Jesus Christ wants to give you victory, but you need to be willing to work at it.

BE MORE AWARE OF THE PRESENCE OF JESUS CHRIST

If Jesus Christ were to appear in your room, what would you do? Masturbate? That would be sick. Well, my friend, He is there, unseen, all the time. Let's become more God conscious.

As you begin to take these simple steps, you will find masturbation having less and less and less of a grip on your life. One day you may wake up in the morning and think, "Wow! I haven't masturbated in weeks!" And really, you haven't even had a desire to do so. Jesus Christ wants to give you victory, but you need to be willing to work on it.

Is it wrong to have strong sexual feelings? Absolutely not! God has made us sexual beings. It is normal to feel strong sexual desires. Instead of ignoring those feelings or pretending they don't exist or trying to run away from them, why not, instead, thank God for them?

Thank Him also for the power that He gives so that you can be in control of this area of your life.

"So I strive always to keep my conscience clear before God and man" (Acts 24:16).

11

Homosexuality
(Is There Hope?)

*Homosexuality is more a matter of what you choose
to do than it is a matter of what you are.* □

"**A**m I gay? 'Cause I'm sure not happy!"
As I travel I run into more and more teenagers
who are being faced with the question of homosexuality. Some are afraid they may be gay. Others have been
approached by strangers, or sometimes even friends,
asking them to become involved sexually.

In this chapter I would like to answer five questions that will help us better understand and cope
with the homosexuality issue.

WHO IS A HOMOSEXUAL?

What are we talking about? Who is a homosexual? Well, *homo* means "same." A homosexual, then,
is someone who is attracted to and excited by members
of the same sex, which leads to involvement sexually
with partners of the same sex. Female homosexuals
are called *lesbians.*

It's really important that we don't confuse homosexuality with love for members of the same sex. It's
important and good and proper to have close, loving
relationships with members of the same sex. Look at
1 Samuel 18:1-3:

After David had finished talking with Saul, Jonathan became one in spirit with David, and he loved him as himself. From that day Saul kept David with him and did not let him return to his father's house. And Jonathan made a covenant with David because he loved him as himself.

David and Jonathan deeply loved each other and were not afraid to show their love. They loved each other in the purest sense of the word. There was no sexual involvement whatsoever.

Let's never let the world so intimidate us that we are afraid to show affection for or have close friendships with the same sex. Don't be afraid to show your love to close friends by giving them a hug. That's good and right, and only the strong can be open like that with their love.

IS HOMOSEXUALITY WRONG?

Is homosexuality wrong? Yes. But when I say that, society becomes extremely angry with me. Why?

Society to a large extent has rejected absolute truth and a personal, all-knowing, all-powerful God who reveals to us that truth and thus gives us a basis for determining right and wrong.

Today we have right and wrong morality that is being decided by the majority. Now if a majority of people can determine what is right or wrong, then truth becomes situational. So what was sinful fifteen years ago may be acceptable today because the majority is making the decision.

On what does the majority base its decisions? Usually upon their feelings, opinions, and thoughts as to what they believe is true and right.

I hope you can see how absurd and dangerous this is. A group now advocates sex with children as a good way to develop closeness between adult and child and to give the child a sense of security. This group's motto is "Sex by eight or its too late!" Now if a *majority* begins to say this is OK, then are incest and sexual relationships with children suddenly right? I hope you are shouting No!

You say to me, "It will never happen, Greg." And I would say to you, "That's what they said about homosexuality twenty-five years ago."

We must take a stand and say clearly that there is a God who has communicated to us absolute truth, that this truth is found in the Bible, and that the Bible is our basis for making decisions about morality. Today we need teenagers who are unashamed to lovingly communicate the truth of God's Word.

I want to speak the truth in love and tell you that homosexuality is not merely an alternative life-style. It is sin. Realize that no amount of legislating, campaigning, advertising, literature, media coverage, or majority acceptance will make it any less a sin.

Nowhere in the Bible does God approve of homosexuality. Let's look at four examples:

□ Leviticus 18:4, 22— You must obey my laws and be careful to follow my decrees. I am the Lord your God . . . Do not lie with a man as one lies with a woman; that is detestable.

□ Leviticus 20:13— If a man lies with a man as one lies with a woman, both of them have done what is detestable. They must be put to death; their blood will be on their own heads.

□ Romans 1:24-27— Therefore God gave them over in the sinful desires of their hearts to sexual impurity for the degrading of their bodies with one another. They exchanged the truth of

God for a lie, and worshiped and served created things rather than the Creator—who is forever praised. Amen.

Because of this, God gave them over to shameful lusts. Even their women exchanged natural relations for unnatural ones. In the same way the men also abandoned natural relations with women and were inflamed with lust for one another. Men committed indecent acts with other men, and received in themselves the due penalty for their perversion.

Some people have tried to water down this passage by saying, "It's only talking about those who are promiscuous. If you have a gay relationship where you are committed to one person, then it's OK."

But that's not what this passage says at all. It says that homosexuality is a perversion, the degrading of your body, shameful, unnatural, and indecent. God doesn't beat around the bush, and neither should we. Homosexual acts in all situations are wrong.

☐ 1 Corinthians 6:9-10— Do you not know that the wicked will not inherit the kingdom of God? Do not be deceived: Neither the sexually immoral nor idolaters nor adulterers nor male prostitutes nor homosexual offenders . . . will inherit the kingdom of God.

That passage says to me that if you continue in the homosexual life-style, you will not inherit the kingdom of God. That is serious and ought to cause you to stop and think. Don't throw away eternity with God in order to live in disobedience for one short lifetime.

Homosexuality is *not* normal. Civilization down through the ages cries out that homosexuality is abnormal. Our race would be extinct if homosexuality were the norm.

Look back to the beginning of God's creation in Genesis 2:18-25. God said, "It is not good for man to be alone." So who did He create? Another man? No, He created a woman. The whole idea of homosexuality just doesn't make sense in the context of God's creation.

Homosexuals will say to me, "It's none of your business what I do, so leave me alone. It's a private act between two consenting adults."

I respond in two ways to that. First, it isn't merely private. It has become public. Because of this private act, we have a public disease known as AIDS that has brought tremendous suffering upon society emotionally, physically, and financially.

Second, the homosexual act is not carried out between consenting adults only. Many, many children are molested, leaving scars that in most cases will last a lifetime. (Let me make clear that heterosexuals also use children sexually, and that too is wrong and sinful.)

The homosexual community would also have us believe that most homosexuals are involved with just one partner. But in reality this seems the exception rather than the rule. Statistics bear that out, and the counseling I have done would confirm that the homosexual is involved with multiple partners.

I talked with an older gentleman who has led a gay life-style. He said that he has had more than 500 different partners and that he knew other men who had been with more than 1,000 partners. What I said to him, and what I would say to you if you're heading in this direction, was, "You deserve better than one-night stands or quick encounters in public bathrooms. People aren't things. We're not merely pieces of meat.

You are somebody special, and God has a better plan for your life than that."

Homosexuality becomes damaging to a person's self-worth. The homosexual loses all self-respect. His conscience becomes seared, but the emptiness and pain remain. Then he tries to escape by more sexual encounters, thinking, *This next one will be different. This encounter will make me happy. Now I'll be fulfilled.*

But he isn't. So he mixes his homosexuality with alcohol and drugs to help soften the emotional pain, and when that doesn't work he seeks the ultimate escape—suicide. The gay life-style isn't.

There can be a lot of excitement and good feelings in a homosexual relationship. (If it didn't feel good, we wouldn't do it.) But the pleasure is temporary and never really satisfies, because the mental, emotional, spiritual, and physical pain outweigh that moment of pleasure.

Homosexuality is wrong. It is a sin, but not greater than other sins. My purpose is not to condemn or destroy you. But I feel it is important that I speak to you the truth in love. Along with that I want to offer you hope:

☐ 1 John 1:7— If we walk in the light, as He is in the light, we have fellowship with one another, and the blood of Jesus, His Son, purifies us from all sin.

Jesus Christ is ready, willing, and able to forgive you and give you a brand new beginning. There is tremendous hope for you if you've been involved in the homosexual life-style.

☐ 1 Corinthians 6:9-11— Homosexual offenders .. [will not] inherit the kingdom of God. And that is what some of you were. But you were washed, you were sanctified, you were justified in the name of the Lord Jesus Christ and by the Spirit of our God.

It's not too late. Even though you have been caught up in the homosexual life-style, you can be washed, cleansed, by the Lord Jesus Christ.

AM I GAY?

Am I gay? Why do teenagers ask me this question? A lot go through what I call homosexual panic. They have had some feelings along this line—perhaps even some experience—so now they are scared to death that they are gay. I tell them, "Relax. Just because you've had certain feelings or even experiences doesn't mean you are homosexual. As a matter of fact, a lot of individuals go through this when they are young. These are some of the typical things I hear:

☐ *"I saw this pornographic magazine with gay individuals, and I got turned on."*
Especially for the male, the visual can be very sexually stimulating. Plus understand that pornographic magazines take "beautiful people," put them in interesting places, and pose them in exciting positions. Their whole goal is to sexually excite you.

Seeing naked people involved sexually can be stimulating no matter what your sex may be, so being excited by some pictures does not mean you are gay.

Realize also that, if this is one of your first exposures to sex, you are attracted to it not because you are homosexual, but because of the initial sexual arousal it caused inside you.

My suggestion is that you stay away from both homosexual pornography and heterosexual pornography.

☐ *"I feel this strong attraction to members of the same sex."*

There is a big difference between being attracted to someone and being involved with that person sexually. The first is temptation; the other is sin. Many individuals at some time in their lives have been attracted to members of the same sex.

☐ *"I actually had a sexual experience with a member of the same sex when I was young, and it excited me."*

God made sex, so it is no surprise that sex is enjoyable. And in the worst of situations there can still be excitement and pleasure. The fact that homosexual sex excited you doesn't make you gay, even though you continue to think about it. You see, we tend to be attracted to and fantasize about experiences we have had.

☐ *"I've been rejected by a member [or members] of the opposite sex, so I guess I was meant to be with members of my own sex."*

Look, we have all been rejected by members of the opposite sex—even me! (How come my wife just rolled her eyes?) It's a fact of life that some people we fall in love with don't love us back. That certainly doesn't make us gay.

My suggestion is that you sit down and talk with someone about this problem. Another person can help you to see things more objectively.

☐ *"I actually had sex with a member of the opposite sex, and I didn't enjoy it that much. So I must be gay."*

Wrong! The media have given us such an unrealistic view of sex and sexual relationships that we feel tremendous pressure. We worry about not measuring up to all the standards of a real man or a real woman. With all these high expectations, it's easy to become disappointed. Realize that for many different reasons sex can initially be embarrassing, uncomfortable, or even painful. Engaging in it before marriage can add guilt, fear, and confusion, which together can make for something quite a bit less than the pure ecstasy you were led to believe you would experience. So here is another good reason to wait until you're older and married!

☐ *"I was physically, emotionally, and/or sexually used and abused by members of the opposite sex."*

I'm sorry for the pain you have gone through. It is understandable that you would be attracted now to members of your own sex. But I want you to know that's a wrong choice, and you can't let those people from your past manipulate you into making a bad decision.

You can't judge an entire sex because of the bad actions of a few. You need to meet some members of the opposite sex who will treat you with love, kindness, and compassion.

It may be that you lack judgment as to what kind of person you should date or spend time with. My suggestion is that you make yourself accountable to your parents and/or other godly men and women. Ask them to screen possible dates and help you to make good choices.

☐ *"People always told me that homosexuality is OK."*

Then I understand how and why you got involved in it, but Jesus Christ says in John 8:32,

"You will know the truth, and the truth will set you free."

The truth is that homosexuality isn't OK, and you need to move away from it.

☐ *"I just don't fit the image of the 'real woman' or the 'real man.' I've just always felt a little different."* There is no set standard for a "real woman" or a "real man." We are all unique creations of God. You don't have to be, nor are you supposed to be, like everyone else. You have special gifts, talents, and abilities. Physically you're supposed to look different from others. People are always coming up to me and saying, "Greg, you look different." (Do you think that's a compliment?)

What I am getting at is don't let anyone tell you that you've got to be this tall, have these measurements, this color hair, or do these certain things to be a "real man or woman." You are a real man; you are a real woman. You are a creation of God Almighty, and that makes you awesome!

Be careful not to fall into another trap: Perhaps people begin to call us names or hint that we may be homosexual. Perhaps lies and gossip are going around. What do we do? Well, we want to prove to others—and in some cases to ourselves—that we aren't homosexual, so we begin to get involved sexually with someone of the opposite sex.

What we find is that, in an effort to take care of our problem, we have only caused for ourselves another problem.

You don't have to prove anything to anybody. The bottom line is that your friends are going to believe you, and those who aren't will find something else to gossip about even if you disprove the homosexuality. So ignore them, be with your friends, trust God to take care of your reputation. And that leads us to the question . . .

WHAT CAUSES HOMOSEXUALITY?

What causes homosexuality? Well, I hear four theories over and over again:

☐ You inherit these tendencies.
    The gay rights movement would like you to believe this. You are born gay, and this is what you will be for the rest of your life. It's part of your makeup. You've got blond hair, blue eyes. You're right-handed, homosexual, and five feet five inches tall. There is little scientific evidence for this.
☐ There's a hormonal imbalance.
    Since each of us has male and female hormones, this could be a possibility. But again the results of research are not conclusive.
☐ There's a spiritual problem.
    If you would just commit your life to Jesus Christ, then you wouldn't have these temptations. Now I agree that the ultimate answer to the needs of man is a personal relationship with Jesus Christ, but I also see man needing help with problems even after he has come to know and love Jesus Christ. A good example of that would be you and the problems and temptations you are still facing in different areas of your life (me too!).
☐ An overwhelming amount of evidence points to the conclusion that homosexuality is a learned behavior.

What factors would lead us toward an attraction to members of the same sex or even to a homosexual life-style? There are many, but let me suggest ten.

☐ First experiences
A first homosexual experience or sexual excitement can lay a foundation for the future. In time our bodies can be programmed to respond and react to certain stimuli. However, if we have taught our bodies to respond to certain stimuli, then we can *reteach* them in time.

☐ Feelings of rejection
Members of the opposite sex have rejected you. You're down, depressed, and you feel "there must be something different about me." Right now you have become very vulnerable to anyone who will appear to love, understand, accept, and reach out to you. So if a member of the same sex begins to express interest, it's easy to see how you would respond.

☐ Unforgiveness
We've been abused in the past, raped, beaten up, torn down emotionally, are victims of incest, or worse. We are unwilling to let go of this hatred and anger by choosing to forgive the offender.

However, the hatred you have toward that person doesn't affect him at all. It just continues to kill you on the inside. So by not forgiving, you are allowing the offending person to continue to abuse and manipulate you emotionally and spiritually.

That hatred will soon turn to bitterness, which will harden your heart. You will then lose your sensitivity to God and His Holy Spirit, which in turn will lead you toward sin. One such sin is hatred toward members of the opposite sex; another would be homosexual relationships. Recovered homosexuals look back and see that the releasing of anger and the offering of forgiveness was the beginning of their healing process.

☐ Fear

What if I fail? Fear of failure is widespread today. Many feel fear in relationships with the opposite sex. What if I don't meet their expectations? What if I make mistakes? What if I don't perform as well as others? What if I really try my hardest but fail anyway? What if I'm not appealing to them? What if they laugh about me? What if they gossip to their friends about me?

We desperately want our basic needs met, and these are to be loved, to belong, to achieve, and then to be recognized for those achievements. So we will turn to those who are meeting those basic needs. The truth is that in the homosexual lifestyle almost everyone is accepted. The "failure rate" is low.

So stop a moment and think. When you find yourself fantasizing about members of the same sex, usually you are not looking for sexual fulfillment at all, but rather for someone to meet your basic need to be loved, to belong, to be accepted, to achieve, and to be recognized. (Want to know a secret? Jesus Christ would like to meet all those needs in your life!)

☐ Poor sex education, or no sex education

If you have been kept in the dark about sex and sexual relationships, you become very vulnerable to an individual or individuals who would lead you toward a homosexual life-style.

Some school sex education programs teach homosexuality as merely an alternative sexual preference. They say they aren't making any moral judgments. But let's be realistic. We both know that if we are teaching homosexuality as an option, then we are putting our stamp of approval on it. Are they teaching sex with children or sex with animals as an option? No. Why? Because they think that is sick behavior, and it is! But you can be sure that if we don't take some stands *now*, our society is heading in the direction of one day teaching adult-child and human-animal sex as two other alternatives.

☐ Excessive self-pity

We fall into a pit of despair. "Nobody really understands me. Nobody really cares. Nobody has had the kind of trauma, pain, and problems that I have had. This is just who I am, so I'll give up and give in to homosexuality."

A person like this usually seeks out others who are like-minded, and you find a lot of this mind-set in the gay movement. We concentrate on the pain of our past, but don't seek to deal with it. Focusing on our pain helps us to rationalize our own sin be-

havior now and justifies our continuing in sin in the future.

☐ Satan.

Just as there is a real God who wants to forgive, love, and set you free, there is also a real devil who wants to bind, use, and destroy you. Satan always seeks to pervert God's good and perfect creation. We are involved in a spiritual warfare, and our battle is not against flesh and blood. We are fighting Satan and his demons.

So next time, don't look at temptation as just a temptation. Think of it as an attack, and start fighting back.

☐ Not really understanding the opposite sex

We are unsure about how the opposite sex thinks, feels, acts, and reacts. We are uncomfortable around them, and that may cause us to say or do stupid things that make us feel awkward. Not really understanding the opposite sex and having had some early bad experiences can push us toward homosexuality.

☐ Poor parental role models

For example, the opposite-sex parent who is abusive physically, emotionally, or sexually can drive the child toward homosexuality. Rejection will do this: "I never wanted you." " I wish you were never born." "Why couldn't you have been a boy?" "Why couldn't you have been a girl?"

Attacking one's sexual identity can lead to homosexuality: "You're not a real man." "You're not a real woman." "Men wouldn't act like that." "You don't act like a woman. No man would ever want you." " What girl is going to go out with you?"

For a man, having a very domineering mother and/or a very weak father can cause anger and fear toward women in general, coupled with a loss of self- respect.

It's interesting and sad to note that very few homosexuals have had good relationships with their fathers.

☐ No personal relationship with Jesus Christ

Without Jesus Christ you really lack the power to do what you know is right. Within the person of Jesus Christ, however, is forgiveness for the past, power for today, and hope for the future.

With Jesus Christ the best is always yet to come. He is waiting, and you don't have to be good enough. You just need to be humble enough to say, "Dear Jesus, please help me, come into my life, forgive my sin, and empower me to live a life that is pleasing to You. I thought I could make it on my own, but I can't."

Without Jesus Christ you really have no strong moral foundation from which to develop your beliefs. But with Christ not only will you discover right and wrong, but you will have new strength through the Holy Spirit to do what is right even when it is difficult.

So What Do I Do?

So you say to me, "OK, Greg, I understand that homosexuality's not right, and it's not good. So what do I do?" Let me suggest some things.

☐ See it as sin.

Stop making excuses, stop rationalizing, stop trying to justify it. Just admit to yourself and God, "You're right. I have been sinning."

Once we are willing to face that, then—Scripture makes clear—we are not to continue in sin. "What shall we say, then? Shall we go on sinning so that grace may increase? By no means!" (Romans 6:1-2). You see, homosexuality is rebellion against God. Your sin is first and foremost against Him. "Against you, you only, have I sinned and done what is evil in your sight" (Psalm 51:4). But at the same time, you are no worse than anyone else. Each of us struggles with sins in a variety of different areas. Remember that those who would look down their noses at you either are intimidated by you and don't really know how to help, or they are hiding some sin themselves.

The fact is that if they had been in your shoes, and had gone through all that you have gone through, they would probably be exactly where you are right now. Ignore them. They, thank the Lord, are in the minority.

In the past you tried to deceive yourself, and you traded God's truth for a lie. But now you're back on the right track.

☐ Come to Jesus Christ.

The hope for you as a homosexual is Christ. Nobody understands as well as Christ understands what you've been through, what you're going through, and what you're going to face.

Hebrews 4:15-16 says: "For we do not have a high priest who is unable to sympathize with our weaknesses, but we have one who has been tempted in every way, just as we are—yet was without sin. Let us then approach the throne of grace with confidence, so that we may receive mercy and find grace to help us in our time of need."

Jesus Christ understands, and He wants to forgive and strengthen you. Some of you have been running a long time, and now you need to come on home.

Our Lord would love to put His arms around you and say, "Welcome home. I've missed you so much."

☐ Each day ask the Holy Spirit to be in control of your life.

In the past you have sought after sin; you have sought to please yourself and others. Now actively seek to please the Lord. The Holy Spirit will give you the power to do that.

Then just take it one day at a time. Wise old Chinese philosopher say, "Trip of one thousand miles begin with first step." The idea is that we live one day at a time, and we don't rely on our own abilities to do what's right. We rest on the Holy Spirit.

You say, "But Greg, right now I am so weak." And my answer is, "Great. Look at Second Corinthians 12:9-10: 'But he said to me, "My grace is sufficient for you, for my power is made perfect in weakness." Therefore I will boast all the more gladly about my weaknesses, so that Christ's power may rest on me. That is why, for Christ's sake, I delight in weaknesses, in insults, in hardships, in persecutions, in difficulties. For when I am weak, then I am strong.' "

☐ Seek the Lord.

Matthew 6:33 says: "But seek first his kingdom and his righteousness, and all these things will be given to you as well."

How do you seek God?

Read and study His Word daily. It will teach, train, rebuke, and correct you so that you are thoroughly equipped for every good work (2 Timothy 3:16-17).

Pray. That is, talk to God. If you're going to have a friendship and love relationship with Christ, be sure you spend time talking with Him daily.

Memorize God's Word. "I have hidden your word in my heart that I might not sin against you" (Psalm 119:11). I believe this is an important key to your gaining victory. The Word of God is powerful. The more you memorize, the more tools you give God for working in your life to build and develop you.

☐ Desire to change.

Ask yourself, "Do I want to change?" The question is not, *Can* I have victory in my life? but, Do I *want* to have victory in my life, and am I willing to take the steps necessary, even though it's difficult?

☐ Get some counseling.

Find or let someone help you find a Christian counselor. Remember, we talked about some of the causes of homosexuality. A good counselor will be able to open your eyes to some of the reasons you are in the shape you're in. You need to look beyond the fact that you are attracted to a member of your own sex to the reasons for that attraction. Please, please, please get some help and counsel. You'll feel so much better, and so will I.

Here is the address of a good organization to get in touch with:

> Exodus International
> Box 2121
> San Rafael, CA 94912
> Tel.415/454-1017

Write or call them. They will be able to help you.

☐ Seek your parents' support.

Your parents can make great friends, and in most cases nobody loves you more then they do, other than God. Maybe you're messed up now because you didn't listen to them. So go back and say,

"I'm sorry for the way I've been, and right now I really need your love, support, encouragement, and wisdom."

Yes, your parents made mistakes, but if you're sharp enough to see all the dumb things they did, then be mature enough to forgive them.

☐ Be vulnerable but cautious.

Ask God to give you the name of one godly man or woman—other than your counselor—that you could confide in. You need a friend to rejoice with and weep with. The encouragement of a friend will be helpful, and it will remove a lot of pressure from you.

You're not looking for another counselor but rather someone who will listen and love you unconditionally. It's important that you talk about and let out all the fears, worries, anger, confusion, and questions that you have. This is a way for you to release pressure between those appointments with the counselor.

I'm not asking you to tell the whole youth group. Just pick a friend. It will probably be better if he or she is several years older than you are. An adult would be good.

☐ Get rid of the garbage.

You know the things that draw you toward a homosexual life-style. You need to get away from these. What might they be?

- Videos
- Magazines
- Parties
- Pictures
- Books

- Letters
- Places
- Friends

Now this last one is one of the hardest things to deal with, but if you're going to make it, you're going to have to sever some relationships. "Do not be misled: 'Bad company corrupts good character'" (1 Corinthians 15:33). It's true, and you have seen it happen.

This will be difficult because for a while you may find yourself alone as you seek a new life-style. But you will discover that God will honor you and that you will gain far more than you ever gave up.

☐ Be encouraged.

The victory is yours. Take hope in the fact that others have gone before you and Christ has set them free.

Second Corinthians 5:17 says: "Therefore, if anyone is in Christ, he is a new creation; the old is gone, the new has come." The homosexual person has passed away. No more do you have to listen to Satan's lies or live in sin.

☐ Be patient with yourself.

Usually no one is harder on us than ourselves. Understand that overcoming will take time. There will still be temptation and maybe even some failure, but don't give up.

You may even find that for a while the temptations will get stronger and sin unusually available. Why? Because you're in a battle, and Satan is trying to pull you back down before you get stronger.

So if things get harder, take courage. That means you're on the right track. Satan is trying to do everything he can to stop you because he knows you are someone valuable and special. Otherwise, he wouldn't bother. So remember 1 John 4:4: "You, dear children, are from God and have overcome them, because the one who is in you is greater than the one who is in the world," and don't give up.

☐ Develop healthy same-sex friendships.

It's good to continue close relationships with members of the same sex, but the key word is *healthy.* Up to this point the relationships have been sexual in nature and therefore unhealthy. You need to discover that you can have a fulfilling, close relationship without sexual involvement.

☐ Right thinking is important.

A process is going on in your life. Whatever you take into your mind goes into your heart, and it is out of the overflow of your heart that you act and speak.

For example, the gay movement would tell you that one out of every ten people is homosexual. You begin to think about that. It starts filling your mind. And then you ask yourself the question, Could I be homosexual?

Now doubt, fear, and confusion flood your mind. The more you think about it, the more you convince yourself that you must be gay.

Then one day your heart overflows with this garbage, and you experiment a little. Suddenly you discover that you can be turned on by a member of the same sex. So that settles it, and you immediately jump to the conclusion, "I am gay." Now you are at least temporarily trapped, and it all goes back to faulty thinking.

So what should I be taking into my mind and dwelling on? "Finally, brothers, whatever is true, whatever is noble, whatever is right, whatever is pure, whatever is lovely, whatever is admirable—if anything is excellent or praiseworthy—think about such things" (Philippians 4:8).

Should we then dwell on homosexuality? Let's find out by asking some questions:

- Is it true? No.
- Is it noble? No.
- Is it right? No.
- Is it pure? No.
- Is it lovely? No.
- Is it admirable? No.
- Is it excellent? No.
- Is it praiseworthy? No.

So should we be taking thoughts of homosexuality into our minds? No. Instead of spending all this time thinking about homosexuality, spend more time thinking about Jesus Christ. Who is He? What is He like? What has He done for you? How can you get closer to Him?

☐ Practice self-control.

Homosexuality is more a matter of what you choose to do than it is a matter of what you are. All of us have to control our sexuality. When you're single, you have to practice self-control and wait to be involved sexually until after you're married. When you're married, you still have to practice self control. You're not to commit adultery. You are to have sexual relationships with your spouse only.

You say, "I'll never be able to fulfill my desires for the same sex." That's true, but remember that those who never marry are not able to fulfill their desires for the opposite sex.

It is possible for you to control those homosexual desires. It's possible for you to develop desires for the opposite sex. "I can do everything through Him who who gives me strength" (Philippians 4:13).

I am asking you to give up the instant gratification that comes from homosexual encounters—a gratification that never lasts—for the much deeper satisfaction of pleasing the Lord.

You can do it. I know you can! How do I know that? Because of what Jude 24 says: "To him who is able to keep you from falling and to present you before his glorious presence without fault and with great joy . . ."

Because God is able!

12

But I've Already Gone Too Far
(Your Options)

"If most of the people around me knew what I've been into, they would just be appalled."

Do you realize that at this very moment some of you are being robbed?

If you came home from a trip to find someone walking out with your TV, how would you react? Would you say, "Hey—channels three and four don't work too good, but five comes in real well. OK, enjoy the TV set." No way! You would stop him.

If somebody reached into your pocket to steal your wallet, what would you do? Would you say, "Hey, that's the wrong pocket. It's over in this pocket. There you go. The credit cards aren't any good, but there is plenty of cash. Good-bye." I don't think so. I bet you would stop him.

Well, some of you are being robbed of the joy, vitality, and abundance that are yours in Jesus Christ.

Now you may ask, "Who's doing the robbing?" I want you to know that it isn't God. In John 10:10 Jesus says, "I have come that they may have life, and have it to the full."

Jesus Christ desires that we experience a full life. It is Satan who seeks to rob us of our joy.

A second question might be: "Why does he want to rob us of joy?" Because what kind of witnesses do we make for Jesus Christ if we approach the world like this: "Hi, I'm a Christian, and I want you to know that it's really depressing. There are so many problems, so many hurts, so many trials. Boy, I can't wait till I die. It would be great to just be dead! Oh, by the way, would you like to become a Christian?"

And what does the world say? "No way. I've got enough problems. I don't need this too."

And finally, you might ask, "How does he rob us of our joy?" I believe one of Satan's most successful tactics is persuading us to zero in on our failures—to focus on the many ways we daily fall short of what we should be. He knows that when we dwell on our failures, that affects not only our view of ourselves but also our view of God. We begin to see Him as one who is disappointed in us and who must reject us because of our sin.

Why do we think that way? Because we've been trained to think that way by the world. If you make a mistake on the job, you expect your boss to be displeased with you. If you work in a shoe store and he asks you to order 100 pairs of size 6 shoes and you order 6 pairs of size 100 shoes, then unless Big Foot happens to walk in the door at that moment, you are in big trouble.

If you make a mistake in the classroom you expect a disapproving glare from your teacher. If you blunder socially, you expect to be rejected. Because of our experience in the world, we think that God must work the same way. He must reject us when we sin. Right? Wrong. That's not true at all! It's time we see sin, failure, and guilt from God's perspective, not the world's.

In Colossians 1:22 we read, "But now he has reconciled you by Christ's physical body through death to present you holy in his sight, without blemish and free from accusation."

When do you become holy, blameless, and beyond reproach? The minute you accept Jesus Christ as Savior and Lord of your life. The price that Jesus Christ paid for you on the cross cleanses you from all sin.

We blow it, sin, fall down, make all kinds of mistakes. But our acceptance with God is not based on how well or how poorly we do. Rather, we are in Christ, and since God accepts Him perfectly, we too are accepted in the Beloved.

There is need to acknowledge the sins you commit, but there is no need to allow them to bind you, control you, totally take you out of service. Let me give you a silly illustration.

You have just been shopping at the mall. Walking across the parking lot to your car, you trip and fall flat on your face! How do you react? You just lie there and say, "Forget it. If I can't walk across the parking lot without falling down, then I quit!" Cars back out and leave, running over you in the process, but there you lie through winter, spring, summer, and fall. You finally shrivel up, and someone comes along and shovels you into a dumpster.

You say, "That's the stupidest thing I have ever heard! If someone falls down in the parking lot, he gets back up." You are absolutely right. Not only would the person get up, but he'd probably get up fast to make sure nobody saw him.

Some of you have been to retreats, spiritual emphasis weeks, evangelistic rallies, and you've got all fired up. You've said, "This time I'm going to be God's man, God's woman. I'm going to follow Him and really allow Him to make a difference in my life." But what happened? You went home and sinned again.

You did some of the very things that you promised God you would never do again. And how did you react? Some of you said, "Forget it. If I can't be a perfect, godly man or woman, then I quit!" Now how stupid is that? When you fall, get back up. Believe 1 John 1:9—"If we confess our sins, he is faithful and just to forgive us our sins and purify us from all unrighteousness." Confess, focus your attention back on the person of Jesus Christ, and keep going.

I am tired of walking down the road of life and having to step over my brothers and sisters who have fallen down on the way and have given up. I don't care what your past has been. It's time to get up. Get up! Get up! Don't just lie there.

I remember an experience from my college days. In the spring, some of the guys would pick a patch of lawn and turn it into a mud hole. Then these guys

would grab some unsuspecting woman on her way to class, carry her over to that mud hole, and drop her in. Now I never ever saw a woman hit that mud and lie in it, saying, "I just love mud." As a matter of fact, they all would immediately crawl out, fighting, scratching, biting, doing whatever was necessary to get out. Nobody ever just sat there in the mud, except on one occasion.

The guys dropped a certain young lady in the mud hole. She tried to get out, but they pushed her back in. She tried to get out a second time, and they pushed her back in. She started to get up a third time, and a guy dumped a wastebasketful of mud over her head. At that point she sat back down in the mud hole and did not move for quite a while.

That well describes our experience with sin. At first, when we have a good relationship with Jesus Christ, we react to sin in the same way we would to that mud hole. We fight; we do whatever we can to get out. But if we allow Satan to push us back in, push us back in, we can eventually sink back into that sin hole and give up. We say to ourselves, "Oh well, I've already gone this far, I might as well go the limit." We give up on God, and we give up on ourselves.

We've got to get out of the mud. We've got to get back on our feet. We've got to allow Christ to forgive us. We've got to step out and be a servant for Him. We are created to live in mansions on high, and some of us are wallowing with the pigs.

But you say, "Wait a second, Greg. You don't understand what I have been involved in. We're not talking about little tiny sins. I mean I have done some real despicable things. I've been incredibly immoral. If most of the people around me knew what I've been into, they would just be appalled. You mean to tell me that God can forgive me?"

And I say to you, "Absolutely! Without a doubt!
Yes!" How do I know that? I know it for two good
reasons.

☐ Number one, God has done it for me.
   There are things I have done in my past that
   have been terrible, but Christ's forgiveness is complete. Even though I fail miserably, He forgives me
   totally.
☐ Number two, He's done it for a famous Bible
   character.
   Remember King David? Do you know what God
   said of King David? "There is a man after my own
   heart!" God dearly loved David. Imagine Jesus
   Christ appearing in your youth group and picking
   out one of the guys and saying, "There is a man
   after my own heart." All of us would be amazed and
   think, "There is someone special." And David was
   someone very, very special. But did David know
   anything about sin? Oh, a little.
      One day while his troops were on the battlefield,
   he wandered out onto his little porch overlooking
   the city. There below him was a woman bathing.
   Now you would think that a man after God's own
   heart would have turned around and walked back
   in and called for his servants. "Cold shower, cold
   shower, cold shower!"
      But David didn't. He stood there and watched
   the woman take a bath, and he lusted after her. He
   said, "Self, I'd like to get to know that woman a
   whole lot better."
      So he sent a messenger down to her house and
   discovered that her name was Bathsheba. The mes-
   senger told Bathsheba, "The king wants to see
   you." Now back in those days, if the king wanted to
   see you, you went! You didn't make excuses and

say, "You know, I'd love to come, but I've got a cake in the oven. I just can't." You went!

So Bathsheba was obedient. She went to King David, and David discovered that Bathsheba was married. Now you would think that a man after God's own heart would have said at this point, "Woops, nice to have you in the kingdom, good to meet you, we'll see you around." But he didn't.

David invited her in. He committed adultery with her, and Bathsheba became pregnant. Now you would think that a man after God's own heart at this point would have confessed his sin. But he didn't.

He developed a scheme to cover what he had done. He called for her husband, Uriah, to come back from the battlefield. "You've done such a good job," he told Uriah, "that I want you to have time at home with your wife."

David was hoping that Uriah and Bathsheba would sleep together so that it would appear that the child was his. But David didn't count on Uriah's loyalty.

"No sir," the soldier replied, "not while the victory is still to be won, and while my fellow soldiers remain on the field!"

Now you would think that a man after God's own heart at that point would be touched and would confess his sin. Well, he didn't.

He wrote a note and said to Uriah, "Give this to your commanding officer when you get back to the front." Uriah was unaware he was delivering his own death sentence. The note essentially said, "Make sure on the next assault that this guy is right in the front. When you engage the enemy, withdraw from him so he is left alone to be killed."

So the next morning Uriah was put on the front line. When Israel met the enemy, his fellow soldiers left him to fight alone—and to die. And what was his crime? His only crime had been that he loved God, was loyal to David, and had a beautiful wife.

Did David know anything about sin? You'd better believe it! He had lusted, lied, deceived, committed adultery, and had an innocent man murdered.

Also, notice how one lie led to another lie, and one sin led to another sin. That's what happens to us, isn't it? We commit a sin, and we try to cover it by telling a lie, which causes us to commit another sin, which means we have to cover our tracks in that area, which causes us to sin again. On and on and on we go until finally we come to repentance.

How much easier it would have been on David, and how much easier it would be on you and me, if we would just admit sins and repent of them at the very beginning, instead of having to go through the whole miserable process.

Did David spend the rest of his life out of fellowship with God? Psalm 130:3-4 says this:

> If you, O Lord, kept a record of sins, O Lord, who could stand? But with you there is forgiveness; therefore you are feared.

In spite of David's gross sins, He found forgiveness. What sin have you committed that God cannot or will not forgive? Jesus Christ took upon Himself all of your sins and my sins. He was willing to die upon a cross so that we could be made right with God. His body was broken so that we could be made whole.

"God made him who had no sin to be sin for us" (2 Corinthians 5: 21).

Too many of us try to die for our own sins. When we make mistakes or fail, we think that by punishing ourselves we will somehow become worthy of Christ's forgiveness.

Understand this: when you try to punish yourself and attempt to pay for your own sin, you really make a mockery of Christ's death. What you are saying is that Christ's death on the cross is really not sufficient to take care of your sins. You need to add something to it. That is sheer folly and one of Satan's most vicious lies.

The price Christ paid for you on that cross is completely sufficient! Nothing needs to be added to it. You can't be good enough to achieve God's acceptance. You can't earn it; you just need to receive it.

We think the issue is whether or not God will forgive us. But that's not the issue at all. The issue is whether or not we will accept His forgiveness and trust Him for the strength and courage necessary to stop sinning.

Jesus Christ has called us to repent of our sins, and repentance does not mean "O God, forgive me so I can go ahead and do it again Friday night." Repentance is being truly sorry for what we've done, agreeing with God that it's wrong, and asking Him for the power to live as He has called us to live.

How did Jesus Christ deal with the woman who was caught in adultery? He said to her, "I don't condemn you. I've come to set you free." But at the same time He didn't say to her, "Now go on back to your adulterous relationship." He said just the opposite, "Go now, and leave your life of sin."

That is what Jesus Christ is saying to us: "I died to set you free. Now go, and leave your life of sin. I've got so many better things in store for you."

Please don't get me wrong. I am not teaching that because of God's forgiveness you now have license to sin. What I am saying is that in Christ we are free to live, to love Him, and to realize that His love for us is unconditional—it is not dependent upon our good performance. This is difficult to grasp because it is so unlike the way we often forgive each other. To illustrate, my beautiful, wonderful wife, Bonnie, is from Southern California. Now it doesn't snow a whole lot in southern California. I married Bonnie and brought her to Rockford, Illinois. On occasion it does snow in Rockford, Illinois.

One winter day shortly after we got married, I came home to discover Bonnie had parked her car on the street. So I drove up the driveway (which was covered by about a quarter of an inch of snow) and into our garage. I went into the house and said, "Hi, honey. How come the car is parked out on the street?"

She said to me, "Well, I was afraid that if I pulled it into the driveway it would get stuck in the snow."

I said to myself, *How cute.* "Listen," I told her, "you don't have to worry. If it snows, just back the car up a little bit, give it some gas, and you'll go right up into the garage."

Some time later Bonnie drove home after our first blizzard. The snow was knee deep in our driveway. Bonnie pulled up to the driveway, looked at it, and said to herself, "Well, Greg said all I have to do is to back the car up, give it some gas, and I'll go right up into the garage."

So my wife backed up our brand new Honda Civic and gave it a little gas (I take that back—she gave it a lot of gas!). As a matter of fact, she probably got going twenty to twenty-five miles per hour and hit that snowdrift. The now airborne Honda Civic landed on a snow pile where it teeter-tottered like Noah's ark on Mt. Ararat.

I came home that evening and could not believe my eyes. It looked like some giant had grabbed our car and thrown it up onto this snowdrift. And there was Bonnie, snow shovel in hand, digging as fast and as frantically as she could. I got out of the car and said, "What happened?"

Bonnie, half hysterical, said, "Well, you told me all I had to do is back up the car, so I backed up the car and went, and I flew, and I'm there, and I don't know what to do!"

Now, if my love for Bonnie was dependent on the way she acted, I would have said to her, "What is wrong with you? Can't you tell the difference between a quarter inch of snow and four feet of snow? That's it. It's over. I want a divorce." But even though at times my wife does silly things, I still love her.

Now the only way I could possibly get this book past my wife to get it published is if I also tell a story about myself. I took Bonnie to see the "Nutcracker Suite." It was close to Christmas and very cold. I waited in line to buy the tickets, while she stood in the lobby with all the other women watching their husbands freeze to death.

Well, I finally got my turn. I bought the tickets, stepped in front of the door, and began to put my money back into my wallet. Now, understand that this lobby is all glass, and there are probably 100 women standing there staring out. I put my money back in my wallet, looked up, and (I have absolutely no idea why I did this) stepped over to the side and walked full blast into one of the plate glass windows. I mean, I didn't have my hand out in front of me to catch myself, and I just smashed my face into this window. With one accord all 100 women broke into laughter.

Now, if my wife's love for me was dependent on the way I acted, I would have walked up to her saying,

"Hi, Honey," and she would have said, "Who's he calling Honey? I've never seen him before." But despite the fact that I do silly things, my wife loves me.

And you see, in spite of the fact that you and I fail, sin, and do foolish things, God still loves us. For He loves Christ, and as believers we are "in Christ."

Now an individual may say, "Wow, that's great! That means that I can sin like crazy Monday, Tuesday, Wednesday, Thursday, Friday, and Saturday, and then come back and gain forgiveness on Sunday." If that is your reaction, I would question your relationship with Jesus Christ. Christians have a love relationship with Him. And love says I desire to do whatever is best for that other individual. I don't want to do anything to use or abuse him.

Imagine yourself out on a date with somebody witty, charming, sophisticated, godly, kind, and incredibly good looking. Now picture a balmy evening, with a full moon. You're walking hand in hand. The person stops, and you turn and gaze at one another. There is a moment of silence, you smile, and your date says, "I love you."

Now what is your reaction to that? Do you say, "Good. From now on I will be rude, crude, ignore you, and act like a slob"? Of course not. Instead, you are so excited that you are loved that you want to do everything you possibly can to please that other person.

Do you mean to tell me that when God looks at you and says, "I love you," your reaction is, "Good. From now on I'll ignore You, take You for granted, blaspheme Your name, and spit in Your face?" The Lord God Almighty, creator of heaven and earth, loves you. That should motivate you to do everything that you can to show love to Him. And then when you do fail, fall, and sin, and confess humbly to God, He says to you, "I understand. I died to forgive it. Get back up and keep on following Me."

Some of you are like prodigal sons and daughters. You've left the Father, and you are wandering on your own. You've been involved in the sin, garbage, and filth of the world. Jesus Christ took care of all your sins at the cross. Your heavenly Father's waiting, and His arms are wide open. It's time you came home. Confess that sin. Turn your back on it. Allow God to wipe it out of your life. He'd like to make you squeaky clean on the inside. Isaiah 43:25—get a Bible and read that verse. Not only are you forgiven, but God doesn't even remember your sins—not because He is stupid or senile but because He chooses to forget. That's how free you are!

Not sure you've ever come to Jesus Christ? Check out chapter 14.

13

Purity
(How to Regain It/How to Maintain It)

Give your body to God right now. ☐

How can I maintain purity? How can I start over again? Those are the kinds of questions I love to hear.

Christ says we are to honor Him with our bodies. "Do you not know that your body is a temple of the Holy Spirit, who is in you, whom you have received from God? You are not your own; you were bought at a price. Therefore honor God with your body" (1 Corinthians 6:19-10). What are some steps we can take to assure that this will happen?

STEP 1

If you have already gone too far, then you need to come to Jesus Christ and gain forgiveness. That's what we covered in depth in the last chapter. It's so important that you come to Him, agree that what you've done is wrong, and desire to honor Him with your body. God desires to separate us from our sins. Psalm 103:12 says, "As far as the east is from the west, so far has He removed our transgressions from us." The wonderful thing about being a Christian is that it's never too late.

You see, Jesus Christ doesn't just see the way things are. He sees what they can be. No matter what your sin or failure, try to see what you could be if you decided to commit your life to Jesus Christ. Up to this point you may have been incredibly immoral. You may have slept with fifty different individuals. But Jesus Christ would like to do something beautiful in and through your life. He sees a diamond, and He wants to make you into a special, godly individual. What's the beginning step, then? Come to Christ on your knees, and repent of your sin.

"If we confess our sins, He is faithful and just and will forgive us our sins and purify us from all unrighteousness" (1 John 1:9).

STEP 2

You need to go to your partner or partners and apologize.

Say how sorry you are that you compromised your relationship with Jesus Christ—that you dishonored Him by your sexual relationship. Say you're sorry for the bad example you have been and that you desire to be different in the future.

Then, you need to apologize for defrauding that other person. God created sex to be shared in a marriage relationship, and you have taken it out of that setting. In a dating relationship, sex causes far more damage than it does good. It is probable that because of your sexual relationships you have left scars on other individuals that will last a lifetime. So you need to apologize for any harm you have done.

STEP 3

If you are going to continue a relationship with that individual, then both of you need to agree to stop the sexual involvement. It is absolutely crucial that you both recognize that the sexual involvement you have had is wrong and that you desire to stop it.

If one says that it is wrong and the other says that it is OK, the relationship will never ever work. Nine times out of ten, the person who has no qualms about sex outside marriage will pull down the other individual.

But let me be up front with you. Once you have tasted of the fruit it is very very difficult to maintain sexual purity. Before experiencing sex you fantasize about what it might be like, but once you have begun to do it, no longer is it fantasy. When you try to stop, all those memories come flooding back at different times. So it is essential that you both agree you need to stop. Otherwise, as a Christian you must break off the relationship.

It boils down to whom you love more. Do you desire to please God or man?

Look at Galatians 1:10. "Am I now trying to win the approval of men, or of God? Or am I trying to please men? If I were still trying to please men, I would not be a servant of Christ."

In this situation you cannot do both! Yes, it will be hard. Yes, there will be tears. But I guarantee that in the long run you will be much better off. And God will bless you because of your courage and convictions.

STEP 4

If you decide to maintain your relationship, or if you are just beginning a relationship with someone else, it's important that you sit down together and set standards. Once a dating relationship begins to get serious, it is healthy to agree on what is proper and what is improper with regard to physical affection. Make clear to one another that love does not use or abuse the one loved, and that you will not go beyond what the set standards are.

If you still do, break off the relationship. Why? Because you really are not loving one another—you are merely lusting. I'm sure your initial reaction to that counsel is, "Oh, he's really being hard." You're right—I am! I think it's time somebody was. It's time you said, "God, I love You so much that I don't want to hurt or disgrace You."

STEP 5

Make sure that God is number one in your life. Matthew 6:33: "But seek first his kingdom and his righteousness, and all these things will be given to you as well."

Seek God first, and He'll take care of your relationships with the opposite sex. When God is number one and you find you aren't dating, instead of getting depressed perhaps you ought to sit back and do a little evaluating. Perhaps you are not dating because you are not ready to date.

If God brought a member of the opposite sex into your life at this point, perhaps you would get involved physically, get your priorities messed up, have problems with your family—all because you have not matured spiritually. Make Jesus Christ number one, seek to be a God-pleaser, and He will take care of the rest.

Making God number one in your life is initially an act of the will. Communicate your desire to God. Tell Him, "Lord, I desire that You become number one in my life. I want to love you more than a boyfriend, girl friend, anyone, or anything." Then that commitment needs to show itself through your actions.

Step 6

Spend time in the Word and in prayer daily. If you expect to have a healthy relationship with the Lord, you must work at it. If you're going to be any good at football, you must practice. If you're going to be any good musically, you must work at it. If you're going to have a life-changing relationship with Jesus Christ, it's going to take some effort on your part.

Listen to Proverbs 7:1-5: "My son, keep my words and store up my commands within you. Keep my commandments and you will live; guard my teachings as the apple of your eye. Bind them on your fingers; write them on the tablet of your heart . . . they will keep you from the adulteress, from the wayward wife with her seductive words."

Being in the Word and in prayer will give you strength and sense to resist the temptations you're going to face.

I would suggest that, once you've been dating for a while, you spend time as a couple in the Word and in prayer. However, I do not recommend that you pray together on the first date.

Now I know that this is radical, but let me explain my reasoning. You kind of like each other. When you see or think about the other person you get those warm fuzzies. Now you're on your first date. He suggests starting the date with prayer (sigh—how wonderful!). You pray together. And feel really good. Then you open your eyes and you look at one another. Do you hear the music building? You take those good feelings God has given you, and you shoot them toward each other instead of back to the Lord.

This experience can cause you to feel a lot closer, more emotionally involved with that individual, than you really ought to be.

So I suggest that you pray and read your Bible before your date. Prepare yourself spiritually for the date just as you prepare physically. Then, after you have dated a while and know that person better, it's great to study the Bible and pray together. Just be sure you transfer those warm feelings the Lord gives you back to Him, not to each other.

Step 7

Something that few teenagers do, but one that is crucial to withstanding temptation, is to memorize Scripture.

Psalm 119:9-11: "How can a young man keep his way pure? By living according to your word. I seek you with all my heart; do not let me stray from your commands. I have hidden your word in my heart that I might not sin against you."

Are you really interested in having Jesus Christ radically transform you? If you are, then let me challenge you to memorize Scripture. When you get into really tough situations the Holy Spirit is there and wants to encourage you. One way He can encourage is by bringing verses to mind. However, He can't very well bring to mind verses that you don't know. Memorizing Scripture will make a big difference in your life.

STEP 8

Be an example as a couple. We desperately need dating couples who are examples of what it means to love Jesus Christ and each other, couples who are morally pure.

Philippians 2:15—"Become blameless and pure, children of God without fault in a crooked and depraved generation, in which you shine like stars in the universe as you hold out the word of life." Jesus Christ would like to make you shine like stars in the universe! As you humble yourself before Him, He would like to display you before men and say, "Look, here are my children. See how they love me? Be like them."

James 4:10, "Humble yourselves before the Lord, and He will lift you up."

Seek out ways in which the two of you can serve Jesus Christ. What might you do together to be involved in service? Ask your youth pastor, pastor, or sponsor for suggestions. Just because you are dating does not mean that you stop serving. Perhaps one thing you can do as a couple is to witness to some of your unsaved friends.

STEP 9

Obey your parents. God works directly through parents, and your response to them is your response to God. I believe that God will give your parents special insight into the individuals that you are dating. You need to seek their advice. If you listen and heed their words, you will save yourself a lot of hurt.

Just in case you don't think you need to be obedient, let me list a few verses you can check out: Ephesians 6:1, Colossians 3:20, Exodus 20:12, Luke 2:51.

It is important that you encourage the person you are dating to develop a good relationship with his or her parents also. Because of you, that guy or girl you are dating ought to be getting closer to his or her parents, not farther away.

I highly recommend that you develop a positive relationship with your parents. One of the key ingredients is communication. Talk with them. Listen to them. Work on your relationship with them.

I also recommend that you spend time as a couple with your parents. That means including them as part of your date sometimes. Perhaps you could all go out to dinner together, or to a ball game. You could go back to the house and spend some time with them. Most young people discover as they get older that parents really do make great friends. Why not develop that friendship now?

I know I am probably old-fashioned, but ladies, you need to be under the authority of your fathers. I believe that if a gentleman would like to take you out on date, he ought to check with your father. Now your initial reaction to that might be, "That is the stupidest thing I have ever heard!" But believe me, in the long run there is great benefit to you. Here are several reasons.

☐ You will discover whether a guy is really interested in you or not.

If you require him to check with your father first, you are going to be able to quickly distinguish between those who may only be interested in your body and those who are really interested in you as a person.

☐ It really takes the pressure off you to make snap decisions.

There you are at your locker, reaching to get your books and run to the next class. All of a sudden you turn around, and there is Harry standing right there, and he asks, "Would you like to go out this Friday night?"

Instead of hemming and hawing under pressure because you've got to get to class, you say to Harry, "Boy, thank you very much. I really appreciate it —but first of all you need to talk with my father."

Give him the telephone number that he can call. In the meantime you can chat with your father, and both of you can come to some decision about Harry. If you would really rather not date him at all, your father is a good one to protect you in that area.

☐ It shows the guy that your father cares about you a lot.

And if guys know your father is that concerned about you, it will gain you far more respect.

STEP 10

It's important to have your date planned. What typically happens is that you don't have to be in until midnight, so you go to a ball game, then out to eat, and it's still only 10:30. Oops! You've run out of things to do! When you have an hour and a half with nothing to do, it's very easy to get involved physically, right? Instead, make sure that you have the date fully planned, but if you do run out of things to do, then choose one of these two options:

☐ End the date.

    Say good night, and each of you go back to your respective places.

☐ Or be alone in a crowd.

    Go to some fast food restaurant, buy a Coke, go to a back booth, and talk. (Have you noticed how few couples are sexually involved at McDonalds?) It gives you the opportunity of talking one to one without the temptations that accompany being totally alone.

STEP 11

Don't set yourself up to fail. Many couples say they want to be different. They want to do what's right. They want to be pure, but they put themselves into situations where they will surely fail in time. You just can't spend hours and hours and hours alone with a guy or girl you are very much attracted to and not expect to have temptation.

Here is what happens. You've got an hour or so before you have to be in, so you say to your date, "Hey, let's pull the car over on this dark road, and we'll just sit here and talk." Well, it sounds like a good idea, and you do talk—for about five minutes. Then you begin to kiss and touch, and soon you are involved physically.

Or you say, "Hey, come on over to the house. My parents are gone, and we have a chance to be alone." Then a favorite suggestion is: "Let's just lie here on the floor together, and we'll watch TV." Stay away from situations where it is very easy to fall.

STEP 12

Beware of dating someone with low moral standards.

"Do not be misled: 'Bad company corrupts good character' " (1 Corinthians 15:33).

It's true that bad company corrupts good character. If you date someone who has low moral standards, chances are he is going to pull you down, rather than your pulling him up. Don't settle for anything less than a godly man or woman. You have trusted Jesus Christ with your eternity; so you can trust Him with your dating relationships. If you will be patient, God will supply!

STEP 13

Don't lose your Christian friends. Too often when we start dating, we develop tunnel vision and blow off the rest of our friends. Don't do that! Balance your time with your friends and the person you are dating. *Listen* to your Christian friends as well. They can see your relationship much more objectively than you can. If they say to you, "This person's a loser," then listen to them. Don't argue. They are your friends, and my guess is that most of the time they are absolutely right.

You say to me, "Oh, Greg, can I really change? Do you know of anybody who has ever had victory in this area?"

I would say to you, "Absolutely." Let me close this book by sharing with you a very special letter.

Dear Greg,

Thank you for your talk on dating and sex. Because of this, my girl friend and I have stopped the physical stuff in time. Praise the Lord, because it is by His power that we can be self-controlled.

It's very hard, because it's not a question of what can I get away with. It's a question of how can I express my love to her in a deeper way. I'm so thankful and full of joy because of your sharing with me from God's Word how to express true love. "I want" doesn't cut it.

She is a very special girl, a true woman of God, and I do love her very much. Selfish fulfillment was tearing us apart from within. But now we have re-established our priorities and standards. It's not easy. We still desire—for lack of a better word—each other very much, but we now have strength and power by virtue of the Holy

Spirit. We will wait until that very special day when we are joined together in perfect union through our Lord Jesus Christ.

I know it won't get any easier, but there is power in prayer, and we love praying to our Father together. I am a weak man, but I have a strong God who lives in me. All praise and glory to the Father through His Son Jesus Christ for now and forevermore. Amen.

Give your body to God right now. Say, "Lord, by Your grace and strength I want to glorify You with my body." It's never too late, no matter how far you've gone. If need be, you now can develop "secondary virginity"—meaning, "I've made a mistake, lost my virginity, but I'm not going to do it again!"

If you have questions, comments, or needs, you can write me. I promise I'll get back to you, if you include a return address.

Greg Speck
c/o Moody Bible Institute
820 N. LaSalle Dr.
Chicago, IL 60610

Don't settle for anything less than God's best. Wait! Why? Because it's worth waiting for.

14

Life That's Worth Living
(How to Belong to Jesus Christ)

*A Christian is someone who has
received Christ into his life.* ☐

Someone may have shoved this book into your hand
and said, "Read it!" You find all this Bible and God
stuff kind of strange. You know something about God,
but you have never met Him personally. I would love
the privilege of introducing you to my Savior, Lord,
and Friend.

But before you can come to Jesus Christ, there are
four things you need to understand.

☐ God loves you.

The Bible says, "For God so loved the world that
He gave His one and only Son. That whoever believes in Him shall not perish but have everlasting
life" (John 3:16).

Understand that God loves you more than anyone has ever loved you in your whole life. He loves
you unconditionally—you don't have to be "good
enough" to be loved by God. He offers you life now
and forever as a free gift.

☐ But there is a problem.

You're aware of the problem—you have sinned.
Again, the Bible says, "All have sinned and fall
short of the glory of God" (Romans 3:23).

219

Sin is disobedience to God, and I know that you are aware of your sins. I didn't get to know Christ until I was a senior in high school. But no one had to tell me I was a sinner. I knew that better than anyone else. Sin separates you from God. So what do we do?

☐ The great news is that Jesus Christ died for all our sins.

"But God demonstrates His own love for us in this: while we were still sinners, Christ died for us" (Romans 5:8).

Christ was willing to hang on a cross for you and me so that our sins could be forgiven. Jesus Christ allowed His body to be broken so that we could become whole! He has made a way for us to be free of our sins and to have close friendship with Him.

☐ It's not good enough to just understand these things.

We have to make a choice: "Yet to all who received Him, to those who believe in His name, He gave the right to become children of God" (John 1:12).

You see, going to church, being baptized, taking Communion, being confirmed, behaving properly—none of these things makes you a Christian. A Christian is someone who has received Christ into his life.

How do you do that? You ask Him through prayer. Have you received Christ into your life? If not, you can do it right now. You could say this:

"Dear Jesus, I know I've made a lot of mistakes. I've made some really poor choices. I've sinned. Thank You for dying for me on the cross. Please forgive me of my sins. Right now I ask You to come into my life. Please take control of my life. Thank

You for forgiving my sins. Thank You for loving me so very much. Thank You for coming into my life. And Jesus, I want You to know that I love You." Amen!

If you meant that prayer, asking the Lord Jesus Christ into your life, you are now a Christian. Write me and let me know of the decision you made, and I will tell you some other important steps that you need to be taking.

And if you and I never ever meet here on earth, someday we will be in heaven together, forever!

IT'S WORTH WAITING FOR in video cassette!

A 2-tape, 4-part series:
(1) Some Straight Talk About Sex (40 min.)
(2) Petting, Pinching, and Peer Pressure (35 min.)
(3) Why Not? (30 min.)
(4) Perversion and Prevention (54 min.)

This video series, priced at $59.95, may be ordered from:

Moody Institute of Science
820 N. LaSalle Drive
Chicago, IL 60610

Moody Press, a ministry of the Moody Bible Institute, is designed for education, evangelization, and edification. If we may assist you in knowing more about Christ and the Christian life, please write us without obligation: Moody Press, c/o MLM, Chicago, Illinois 60610.